Global Stock Markets and Portfolio Management

Centre for the Study of Emerging Markets Series

Series Editor: **Dr Sima Motamen-Samadian**

The Centre for the Study of Emerging Markets (CSEM) Series provides a forum for assessing various aspects of emerging markets. The series includes the latest theoretical and empirical studies from both academics and practitioners in relation to the economies and financial markets of emerging markets. These cover a wide range of subjects, including stock markets and their efficiency in emerging markets, forecasting models and their level of accuracy in emerging markets, dynamic models and their application in emerging markets, sovereign debt and its implications, exchange rate regimes and their merits, risk management in emerging markets, derivative markets and hedging decisions in emerging markets, and governance and risk in emerging markets.

The series is one of the main sources of reference on emerging markets, both within and outside those markets, for academics, national and international agencies, and financial institutions.

Titles include:

Sima Motamen-Samadian (*editor*)
DYNAMIC MODELS AND THEIR APPLICATIONS IN EMERGING MARKETS

CAPITAL FLOWS AND FOREIGN DIRECT INVESTMENTS IN EMERGING MARKETS

RISK MANAGEMENT IN EMERGING MARKETS

GOVERNANCE AND RISK IN EMERGING AND GLOBAL MARKETS

ECONOMIC TRANSITION IN CENTRAL AND EASTERN EUROPE

GLOBAL STOCK MARKETS AND PORTFOLIO MANAGEMENT

ECONOMIC AND FINANCIAL DEVELOPMENTS IN LATIN AMERICA

Also by Sima Motamen-Samadian:

INTERNATIONAL DEBT AND CENTRAL BANKING IN THE 1980s (*edited with Z. Res*)

EMERGING MARKETS
Past and Present Experiences, and Future Prospects (*edited with C. Garido*)

Centre for the Study of Emerging Markets Series
Series Standing Order ISBN 1–4039–9521–4

You can receive future titles in this series as they are published by placing a standing order. Please contact your bookseller or, in case of difficulty, write to us at the address below with your name and address, the title of the series and the ISBN quoted above.

Customer Services Department, Macmillan Distribution Ltd, Houndmills, Basingstoke, Hampshire RG21 6XS, England

---

Global Stock Markets and Portfolio Management

Edited by

Sima Motamen-Samadian

palgrave macmillan

First published 2006 by
PALGRAVE MACMILLAN
Houndmills, Basingstoke, Hampshire RG21 6XS and
175 Fifth Avenue, New York, N.Y. 10010
Companies and representatives throughout the world.

PALGRAVE MACMILLAN is the global academic imprint of the Palgrave Macmillan division of St. Martin's Press, LLC and of Palgrave Macmillan Ltd. Macmillan® is a registered trademark in the United States, United Kingdom and other countries. Palgrave is a registered trademark in the European Union and other countries.

ISBN-13: 978–1–4039–9155–3
ISBN-10: 1–4039–9155–3

This book is printed on paper suitable for recycling and made from fully managed and sustained forest sources.

A catalogue record for this book is available from the British Library.

Library of Congress Cataloging-in-Publication Data
Global stock markets and portfolio management / edited by Sima Motamen-Samadian.
p. cm.—(Centre for the Study of Emerging Markets Series)
Includes bibliographical references and index.
ISBN 1–4039–9155–3 (cloth)
1. Stock exchanges – Econometric models – Case studies.
2. Portfolio management – Econometric models – Case studies.
3. Capital movements – Developing countries – Econometric models.
4. Investments – Developing countries – Econometric models.
I. Motamen-Samadian, Sima. II. Series.
HG4551. G637 2006
332.64—dc22 2005044515

10 9 8 7 6 5 4 3 2 1
15 14 13 12 11 10 09 08 07 06

Printed and bound in Great Britain by
Antony Rowe Ltd, Chippenham and Eastbourne

Contents

List of Figures and Tables

Figures

Tables

Preface

In the growing globalized financial markets of today, investors are increasingly searching for new markets that can offer better investment opportunities. Theoreticians have long been highlighting the gains from international portfolio diversification. The high level of capital flows across the world in recent years is a clear indication of the extent to which investors are seeking to expand their scope and include a wide range of financial assets from different parts of the world in their portfolio. Despite gains from international diversification, investors remain concerned about unanticipated changes in stock prices in newly developed markets and tend to approach those markets with great care. Empirical studies on specific features of emerging stock markets, therefore, can not only help international investors in their decision making, but can also guide the host markets in fine tuning their policy designs and regulations.

The six studies included in this volume provide a new insight into the similarities and differences between the behaviour of stocks in emerging and developed markets, and into the implications of their inclusion in a portfolio of international investors on the overall return of the portfolios. Following Chapter 1, an overview of the volume, Chapter 2 provides an analysis of the behaviour and exposure of hedge funds in 26 emerging markets in Latin America, Asia and Eastern Europe, prior to and following the 1997 Asian currency crisis. Chapter 3 uses threshold and exponential GARCH models to examine stock price responses in five Middle Eastern and North African (MENA) markets to news of unexpected inflation. Chapter 4 examines the prospects and implications of financial integration of the MENA markets into the global markets, and shows how the Gulf Cooperation Council (GCC) equity markets can still offer potential for portfolio diversification. Chapter 5 looks at the dynamic linkages between crude oil price shocks and stock market returns in 21 emerging markets and Chapter 6 provides an assessment of the implications of regulatory changes in China's stock market. Finally, Chapter 7 tests the efficiency of the Warsaw stock markets, and demonstrates the possibility of deriving some optimal investment strategies that can generate abnormal profits.

Overall, the studies make a valuable contribution to the existing literature on global portfolio management, and provide interesting information about some of the markets that are still new to many investors.

SIMA MOTAMEN-SAMADIAN

Acknowledgements

This volume is a collection of some of the papers presented at the International Conference on Emerging Markets and Global Risk Management in June 2004 in London. The conference was organized by the Centre for the Study of Emerging Markets (CSEM) at the Westminster Business School. In this respect, my sincere thanks go to Hanna Scobie at the European Economic and Financial Centre, who inspired and supported me in organizing the conference.

My special thanks go to all the contributors for their timely delivery of the chapters and to Jacky Kippenberger and Rebecca Pash at Palgrave Macmillan for their patience and support during the production of this book. I am also indebted to my family and, in particular, to my husband Vahab Samadian for his constant support while I was working on the book.

SIMA MOTAMEN-SAMADIAN

Notes on the Contributors

Samer A.M. Al-Rjoub is a Professor of Finance in the Department of Banking and Finance at Hashemite University, Jordan.

Jing Kong is a Researcher in Finance in the Department of Economics at the National University of Singapore, Singapore.

Ding Lu is a Professor of Economics at the National University of Singapore, Singapore, and at Sophia University, Japan.

Aktham Maghyereh is a Professor of Finance in the Department of Banking and Finance at Hashemite University, Jordan.

Guillaume Monarcha is a Researcher in Finance at the CEFI and Assistant Professor of Economics and Finance at the University Aix-Marseille 2, France.

Sima Motamen-Samadian is Director of Centre for the Study of Emerging Markets and a Principal Lecturer in Economics at the Westminster Business School, University of Westminster, United Kingdom.

Simon Neaime is a Professor of Finance in the Department of Economics, at the American University of Beirut, Lebanon.

Robert Ślepaczuk is a researcher and part-time lecturer at Warsaw University, Poland.

1
Introduction

Sima Motamen-Samadian

The integration of emerging markets into global financial markets has extensively improved the scope for the optimal allocation of assets across many countries. Following the 1997 East Asian currency crises, and the subsequent financial crises in Russia, Brazil, and Argentina, a number of investors considered the risks and uncertainty concerning future developments in those markets too high and returned to well established developed markets to diversify their portfolios. In the aftermath of the drop in yield of western stock markets, however, fund managers are once more considering investment in emerging markets in search of higher rates of return; they are ready and keen to reshuffle their portfolios in their favour, though with some caution.

Generally, investors aim at minimizing the risks and maximizing the expected value of their portfolios. Theories of portfolio management all support the view that a globally diversified portfolio that includes stocks in a variety of geographical locations and sectors can provide higher rates of return. Such diversifications can be more attractive if investors are able to access to greater information about the responsiveness of financial assets to various factors, such as change in regulations or various macroeconomic indicators. Therefore, more detailed knowledge of the behaviour of stocks in various markets can help investors to better manage their portfolios.

Most theories of portfolio decision making have been developed on the basis of features of developed stock markets rather than those of emerging markets. It is necessary for investors who wish to invest in emerging markets to appreciate the heterogeneous features of those markets and the way they might respond to various factors.

This volume is designed to provide a better understanding of the type of risks and returns that investors might face in various emerging markets, and the usefulness of some of the existing models in managing portfolios in those markets.

In Chapter 2 Guillaume Monarcha examines the behaviour of 26 hedge funds in emerging markets, both prior to and following the 1997 Asian currency crisis. In order to estimate the exposure of hedge funds, Monarcha develops a multifactor model that includes returns from bond, equity and currency indices. He then uses a stepwise selection procedure, and finds that equity indices in all of the 26 funds in Latin America, Asia and Eastern Europe exhibited positive and low leveraged exposure to emerging equity factors, and heterogeneous significant exposure to other factors. Monarcha uses the random walk version of the Kalman filter to estimate the time varying exposure of emerging markets hedge funds. By analyzing the dynamics of the coefficients during the Asian currency crisis of 1997, he finds that most hedge funds that exhibited significant exposure to the Asian factors reduced their exposures after the crisis. He furthermore finds that many of the funds that were exposed to Latin American and Eastern European markets reacted heterogeneously to the crisis after June 1997, irrespective of whether they had been exposed to Asian factors or not.

In Chapter 3 Samer A.M. Al-Rjoub, provides a study of the Middle East and North African (MENA) markets and examines the response of stock prices in Bahrain, Egypt, Jordan, Oman and Saudi Arabia to information about inflation. Here, the author tries to analyze the reaction of monthly stock returns to the unexpected portion of the Consumer Price Index (CPI) inflation rate, and assesses how unexpected inflation can cause asymmetric shocks to the volatility of stocks in those countries. To capture the news effect of unexpected inflation, Al-Rjoub uses threshold and exponential GARCH models, and finds a negative and strongly significant relationship between unexpected inflation and stock returns in those markets. His results also indicate that there appears to be no asymmetric news effect in the listed stock markets of the MENA countries and that they do not exhibit much volatility.

In Chapter 4, Simon Neaime, examines the prospects and implications of the global integration of the Middle Eastern and North African (MENA) stock markets, and explores whether these markets can offer a unique risk/return feature to international investors for portfolio diversification. His cointegration tests reveal that while some of the MENA stock markets such as Egypt and Jordan have matured and are now integrated with the world financial markets, there are still some (such as the Gulf Cooperation Council (GCC) equity markets) that can offer potential for portfolio diversification through mainly mutual funds. Neaime also carries out some Granger causality tests that offer weak evidence for regional financial integration, except among the GCC stock markets.

Aktham Maghyereh, in Chapter 5, tries to assess the dynamic linkages between crude oil price shocks and stock market returns in 21 emerging countries in Latin America, Eastern Europe, Asia, and the Middle East and North Africa. Here, the author uses vector autoregressive (VAR) analysis on daily data for the period 1 January 1998 to 31 April 2004. To forecast error variance decomposition and impulse response, Maghyereh uses the generalized approach to VAR instead of the more traditional orthogonalized approach. His study shows that contrary to earlier findings on developed markets, oil shocks appear to have no significant impact on stock index returns in emerging economies. The results also suggest that stock market returns in these countries do not rationally signal shocks in the crude oil market.

Chapter 6 is devoted to study of Chinese stock markets, where Jing Kong and Ding Lu assess the impact of regulatory changes on the A and B share markets that cater mainly for domestic and foreign investors respectively. The authors group the regulatory changes and policy adjustments in China's stock market into six major categories, and use a modified ARIMA outlier detection methodology on the data for the period 1995–2003 to identify large shifts of market returns in the sub-markets. Their study reveals that all outlier returns tend to be temporary, with most coinciding with the days around the events. Estimation of a modified GARCH-M model indicates remarkable asymmetric market reactions to certain categories of events. For instance, the B-share market not only displayed much stronger reactions to market-boosting news, but also reacted before the news was announced. As for expansion in market size, investors seemed to respond negatively to expansion of the A-share market but positively to that of the B-share market. Kong and Lu's observations also suggest that the regulatory constraint on the floating range of stock has been associated with reduced volatility in the A-share market but not so in the B-share market. Both markets, however, appeared to behave with greater volatility the day after long public holidays. Their results may not only provide useful tips to investors, but also reveal some institutional features of China's stock market development.

Finally Robert Ślepaczuk in Chapter 7 attempts to verify the validity of the weak form of efficient market hypothesis (EMH) in the case of Polish stock markets, by examining the possibility of deriving an investment strategy that can 'beat the market'. In testing the EMH, Ślepaczuk uses the available data on the main derivatives quoted on the Warsaw Stock Exchange. This is a departure from the other tests of EMH in the literature. He first creates detailed buy/sell signals for investment strategies, and then shows that it is possible to use historical data and optimize parameters of some of the tools used in technical analysis (moving averages, oscillators, directional movement indexes, volume based techniques, etc.) to determine an investment strategy that can generate abnormal returns. The optimization results, based on average daily and weekly rates of return, thus revealed the possibility of rejecting Fama's weak-form of EMH. Ślepaczuk argues that this 'beat the market strategy' may be produced due to differences that as yet exist between the characteristics of developed and emerging markets.

2

The Dynamics of Emerging Markets Hedge Funds Exposures during the Asian Currency Crisis of 1997

Guillaume Monarcha

Introduction

During the last decade, hedge funds attracted the attention of the financial community for two major reasons: their capacity to generate superior performance, and their lack of transparency. However, since the market events of the 1990s, they are frequently associated with managers such as George Soros, who is well known to have taken considerable advantage of the European currency devaluations in 1992. Following the Asian currency crisis of 1997, the good reputation of hedge funds has been greatly damaged. They were suspected of having been an active contribution to the trigger of the speculative attacks that led to the Ringgit and Baht devaluations. Academics then assumed that hedge funds might be capable of disrupting financial markets through an intensive use of leverage and derivatives. This atmosphere of suspicion was reinforced by the collapse of long term capital management in 1998. Once more, an isolated event attracted regulators' attention.

The vector of these strong reactions, which led to misleading generalizations, is certainly the lack of transparency. In fact, the commonplaces concerning the hedge funds industry are often erroneous.

Nevertheless, works have been carried out in order to determine the role that hedge funds played during the 1990s market events. For example, Corsetti *et al.* (2004) show that in the presence of one highly leveraged institution (i.e. a hedge fund) a currency crisis may occur in a small country even if the fundamentals of the country are acceptable.

Several empirical works have been undertaken in order to test this assumption, but as yet it remains unconfirmed. Brown, Goetzman and Park (1998) tested the hypothesis that ten global macro funds may have caused the Asian currency crisis.[1] They found no evidence of major bets against the Asian currencies and concluded that global macro funds were not responsible for the crisis. Eichengreen and Mathieson (1998) arrived at similar conclusions. They found that some hedge funds bet against the Baht around the time of the crisis, but they made it clear that hedge funds' exposures were not sufficient to destabilize Asian markets. Furthermore, they noticed that negative feedback trading strategies used by certain managers may have limited the extent of the damage. Fung and Hsieh (2000) and Fung, Hsieh and Tsatsaronis (2000) tested certain propositions formulated by Eichengreen and Mathieson (1998). They considered that investors such as hedge funds may create sources of market disruption in three cases: if they take important short positions, if they use positive feedback trading strategies or if they herd. They concluded that hedge funds were not responsible for the Asian currencies devaluation (they had no important short positions before the crisis) and that they did not magnify the crisis (apparently, they used contrarian strategies rather than positive feedback trading). They found similar results concerning other market events, with the exception of the EMU crisis of 1992 where the implication of the Soros Quantum Fund is quite clear.

According to these authors, it is obvious that the hedge funds industry did not necessarily play a major role in all recent incidences of currency turmoil. Nevertheless, one point drew our attention. All issues that deal with the market impact of hedge funds are based on the same problematic: Do hedge funds cause market disruptions? Even so, it would be pertinent to reverse this causality effect; that is, to consider the following problematic: Do major market events affect hedge funds investment policy? To our knowledge, the only academic work that approaches this issue with a similar problematic was carried out by Eichengreen and Park (2002). They investigated the effects that long term capital management failure may have had on the use of leverage in the hedge funds industry. Their findings showed that credit lines raised by managers decreased following this event.

In this chapter, we focus on a connected problematic: identifying the changes that occurred in emerging markets hedge funds strategies after the Asian currency crisis of 1997. We concentrate our analysis on this market event because of its importance and the attention that it attracted among the politic, regulatory and academic communities. It differs from the works cited above in that we only consider emerging markets hedge funds because, unlike other hedge funds categories, they invest in these markets in a systematic way. We then suppose that they were investing in emerging markets assets before and after the crisis; that is certainly not the case for other hedge funds, which mainly made opportunistic bets during the crisis (if at all).

Our approach comprises two steps. First, we identify the individual strategies followed by the 26 emerging markets hedge funds for which we obtained data (from February 1995 to December 1999). Second, we analyze the dynamics of their strategies; that is, the changes in their market exposures during and after the crisis.

Emerging markets hedge funds

The wide diversity of investment strategies used by hedge funds and the lack of a unified legal framework make it difficult to define hedge funds absolutely. However, they have common characteristics:

- The term 'hedge fund' refers to a private investment pool, managed by professionals and not freely accessible to any investors. It may be situated offshore. Hedge funds are exempt from legal obligations concerning investors' protection. For example, they are not subject to the Investment Company Act 1940.
- Hedge fund investors may be high net worth individuals or institutional investors such as commercial banks, mutual funds, pension funds or insurance companies. They are quite elitist in the way in which they select potential investors: eligibility may be determined by the amount of capital invested (which must exceed a minimum amount settled by the manager – sometimes in excess of one million US$). Furthermore, the investment is subject to a redemption period (which can vary from a few months to several years) in order to limit the fund's liquidity constraints.

- Hedge funds may freely use leverage, short sales, repos and derivatives. These practices are limited by the manager's internal risk management policy and the counterparties' requirements.
- Another hedge funds particularity is the fee structure of the fund. First, any investor must pay an entrance fee, which can vary from 1 to 2 per cent of the capital invested. Second, managers' fees are based upon incentive and usually vary from 15 to 20 per cent. As this type of fee structure may decrease managers' risk aversion, most hedge funds set up high-water marks.[2]

Although hedge funds have common characteristics, they differ as to the investment strategies they use. These strategies depend on several factors. They may be directional or non-directional, request a variety of investment instruments (which may be derivatives or more conventional asset classes) and may be focused on specific geographical zones.

Emerging markets hedge funds investments should mainly be orientated towards emerging markets (i.e. South Asia, Eastern Europe and Latin America). They may invest in several asset classes (equities, bonds, interest rates, foreign exchange). But even if hedge funds have the opportunity to use derivatives and to take short positions without any constraints, they should be limited concerning emerging markets. Indeed, repos or other derivatives are quasi-inexistent or may suffer from a high lack of liquidity in these markets.

Following on from this point, we may find low leveraged exposures to emerging equity markets (positive and less than unity). This would probably involve positive or negative exposure to less risky asset classes (for example, developed markets bonds and stocks) in order to mitigate risks involved by emerging markets exposures (such as currency risk, credit risk, liquidity risk, political risk and systemic risk).

Identifying emerging markets hedge funds strategies

In our work, we use emerging markets hedge funds data extracted from the TASS database. As available data are collected from self reporting, hedge funds managers generally disclose limited information, such as the fund's strategy (long/short equity, fixed income or emerging markets, for example), average leverage, asset classes traded (securities, bonds or currencies) and monthly returns.

Our aim is to identify asset classes to which the funds are exposed (Asian equity market, Latin American bonds, and so on). The difficulty with the identification of hedge funds strategies, therefore, is the extraction of exposures to different asset classes from returns. A standard solution for this problem is to use multifactor models.

The model

Generally, multifactor models designed for hedge funds are formulated as follows:

$$R_{i,t} = \alpha_i + \sum_{j=1}^{J} \beta_{i,j,t} + \varepsilon_t \qquad (2.1)$$

In this equation, $R_{i,t}$ denotes the i fund return at time t, $\alpha_{i,t}$ is a constant, $r_{j,t}$ is the return on factor j at time t, $\beta_{i,j,t}$ represents the i fund return sensitivity to factor j at time t and ε_t is the error term.

The constant term can be compared to the part of the return systematically generated by the manager. The error term represents the risk specific to the manager's stock picking ability. Unlike the coefficients of the Sharpe (1992) style analysis model, $\beta_{i,j,t}$ coefficients may be positive or negative (to take into account short positions) and may be higher than unity (to take into account the use of leverage).

Factors included in the model are emerging markets hedge funds factors identified in Monarcha (2004). These are monthly returns on emerging markets equity indices (ASIA for Asia, AMLAT for Latin America and EUREST for Eastern Europe) and returns on emerging markets bond indices (BAS for Asia, BAL for Latin America and BEE for Eastern Europe). We also include returns on three emerging markets currency baskets (CAS, CAL and CEE for Asia, Latin America, and returns on developed countries' equity and bond indices.[3] Dependant variables are the monthly returns of 26 emerging markets hedge funds (EM1 to EM26).

We use a stepwise selection procedure, a method that it is quite fast and reliable, which permits us to avoid multicolinearity problems. We estimate the model for the period February 1995–November 1999.

Estimation results

Regressions results are summed up in Tables 2.1 and 2.2. Complete results are exposed in Table 2A in the Appendix. We found an average R-squared of 0.67, which points out that the factors included in the model are quite representative of emerging markets hedge funds risk exposures. Implicitly, this suggests that the lack of liquidity and the high volatility of emerging equity markets can be a brake to the setting up of dynamic trading strategies. In this case, estimated R-squared would have been lower.

Table 2.1 Summary statistics of emerging markets hedge funds estimated exposures

1.a – Assets traded*		**1.b – Zones***		**1.c – Total exposure****	
Equities	60 (96)	Asia	18 (38)	< 1	23
Bonds	32 (54)	Latin America	34 (72)	[1;2]	54
Currencies	8 (19)	Eastern Europe	34 (62)	> 2	23
		Dvp. countries	14 (35)		

Notes: * in % of the estimated exposures (% of funds)

** % of funds. Total exposure = $\sum_{i=1}^{n} |\beta_i|$

Table 2.2 Coefficients statistics

	No. of funds	Positive	Negative	Mean	Median	Minimum	Maximum
CST	26	21	5	0.00	0.00	−0.04	0.04
AMLAT	16	16	–	0.68	0.74	0.22	1.10
ASIA	10	9	1	0.29	0.22	−0.23	1.01
EUREST	10	10	–	0.29	0.23	0.08	0.63
BEE	10	9	1	0.36	0.46	−0.51	0.71
JPMGGBI	6	–	6	−1.26	−1.02	−3.05	−0.45
MSCIWI	3	2	1	0.22	0.34	−0.37	0.69
CAL	3	3	–	1.06	1.02	1.01	1.14
BAL	3	2	1	0.12	0.66	−1.27	0.95
CEE	2	–	2	−0.82	−0.82	−1.10	−0.54
BAS	2	–	2	−0.51	−0.51	−0.71	−0.32

All 26 hedge funds are highly exposed to emerging markets assets, particularly to Latin American and Eastern European markets. We identified 10 Asian funds; that is, 10 funds that are exposed to Asian assets (bonds, equities or currencies).

We also notice that equities are apparently present in almost all hedge funds portfolios, thus being the most traded asset class with 60 per cent of the estimated exposures. Bonds related factors are also relevant, being traded by more than one half of the funds and representing 32 per cent of the exposures.

The low exposure to currency factors (only 8 per cent) shows that emerging markets hedge funds mainly take unhedged positions. Effectively, equity and bond based factors are US dollar denominated. That implies, for example, that a hedged position in Asian equities might be associated with a negative exposure to the Asian currency basket, which is not the case of most emerging markets exposures.

Another point to note is the estimated leverage (which is approximated by the sum of the absolute betas). We notice that most hedge funds exhibit low leverage (77 per cent of the funds have a total exposure below 2). This result is consistent with our hypothesis concerning emerging markets hedge funds: the lack of derivatives that may be traded on emerging markets limits the use of leverage.

A striking result is emerging markets hedge funds' exposure to equity factors in Asia, Latin America and Eastern Europe. Coefficients associated with AMLAT, EUREST and ASIA are quasi-systematically positive and rarely higher than unity (with a maximum of 1.10).

Estimated exposures to bond indices are more heterogeneous than equities exposures. On the one hand, we observe that all of the 10 funds exposed to the Eastern European bond market hold long positions (coefficients varying from 0.08 to 0.63). On the other hand, exposure to the Asian and Latin American bond markets vary from −1.27 to 0.85. This point is not inconsistent in view of our assumptions. Actually, emerging bond markets are much more liquid than emerging equity markets. They offer more opportunities to hold short positions (via derivatives). Negative exposures to emerging bonds may be used to offset country risks involved by large positive exposures to emerging equities.

Our findings are consistent with our assumptions regarding strategies followed by emerging market hedge funds. They use low leverage and mainly follow passive buy and hold strategies on emerging equity markets; their exposure to bond markets may be positive or negative on both emerging and developed markets.

Estimating the dynamics of hedge funds exposures

Brown, Goetzman and Park (1998) estimated the variations in hedge funds exposures using a rolling regression procedure with a four-month window. But as Brealey and Kaplanis (2001) pointed it out, the variations of the coefficients were considerable because of the small number of observations used to estimate the model. The major problem of this approach is the size of the window used. Generally, when the time window is short, the estimated coefficients are variable.

Another problem is that in the presence of heterogeneous funds (which is the case for hedge funds), we need to adapt the size of the window to the investment policy of each fund. Effectively, as pointed out by Swinkels and Van der Sluis (2002), funds that change their exposure frequently would require a relatively small window (thus generating high variability in coefficients) whereas those with a longer horizon of investment would require a larger window. To avoid this problem, the estimation of a dynamic linear model seems more judicious.

Formulating dynamic exposures

We modify the static model defined by equation (2.1) in order to incorporate varying time coefficients:

$$R_{i,t} = \alpha_i + \sum_{j=1}^{J} \beta_{i,j,t} + \varepsilon_t \qquad (2.2)$$

$$\alpha_t = c \qquad (2.3)$$

$$\beta_{i,j,t} = \beta_{i,j,t-1} + \mu_{i,j,t} \qquad (2.4)$$

where $\varepsilon_i \sim NID(0;\sigma^2_\varepsilon)$ and $\mu_i \sim NID(0;\sigma^2_{\mu,i})$

We suppose that α_i is time invariant, which implies that we consider the value added by a manager's ability to be constant over time. We also assume that the $\beta_{i,j,t}$ coefficients follow a random walk process. This means that the model allows for fundamental changes in the strategic lines followed by the manager. Actually, it is quite probable that the strategy of a fund may vary according to market events, such as volatility increase or financial crisis. Strategic variations will then occur with shocks generated by the random variables $\mu_{i,j}$.

Equations (2.2) to (2.4) form a dynamic linear model, in which equation (2.2) is the signal equation. Equation (2.3) and the set of equations defined by (2.4) are the transition equations. Such a model can be estimated with the Kalman filter algorithm, as described in Harvey (1989) and Newbold and Bos (1985). To do so, we must develop certain technical points.

We rewrite the model as follows:

$$R_t - c = C_t B_t + \varepsilon_t \tag{2.5}$$

$$B_t = A_t B_{t-1} + \omega_t \tag{2.6}$$

where, B_t, C_t, and ω_t are vectors of dimension J, respectively for the coefficients, the factors and the shocks in the transition equations. A_t is a $J \times J$ matrix.

We suppose that the shocks in the transition equations are independent, which implies that their covariance matrix is diagonal. In equation (2.4), we also assume that the $\beta_{i,j,t}$ are independent, thus implying A_t to be an identity matrix and that the μ_i are also independent in turn implying that the covariance matrix of the ω_t's is diagonal. Furthermore, the use of the Kalman filter requires parameters initialization, especially for the states covariance matrix. We set initial states to zero and states covariance to 10^6.

The variations in hedge funds exposures around the Asian currency crisis of 1997

As shown before, emerging markets hedge funds are mainly exposed to emerging equity markets. We thus suppose that changes in their strategies following the Asian currency crisis will be entirely reflected by changes in their exposures to the corresponding factors. In our analysis, we distinguish three periods: a pre-crisis period (from October 1996 to May 1997), a crisis period (from June 1997 to January 1998) and a post-crisis period (from February 1998 to September 1998).

Although Figure 2.1 shows that the Asian equity market was affected by the crisis until July 1998, we limit the crisis period to the

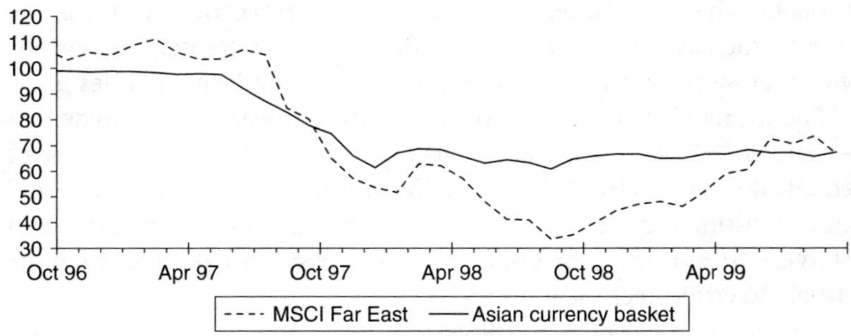

Figure 2.1 Asian markets' performance around the Asian currency crisis

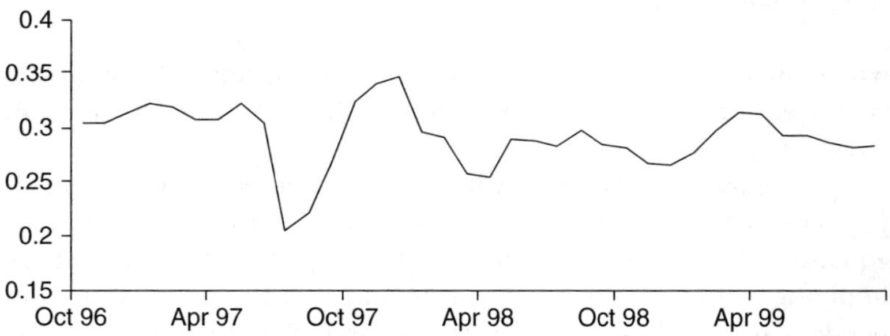

Figure 2.2 Mean estimated exposure to Asian equities

currency devaluation period; that is, between June 1997 and January 1998. We then suppose explicitly that the Asian equity market disruptions that occurred after July 1998 are a consequence of the crisis rather than its manifestation. In the same way, we limit the post-crisis period to September 1998 for two reasons. First, the extension of this period would have implied that the coefficients' dynamics would have been affected by the Russian crisis episode. Second, there is little chance that hedge funds exposures remain unchanged in the long run, thus justifying a relatively short post-crisis period.

Figure 2.2 shows the evolution of the mean exposure to the Asian equity market.[4] We note that hedge funds exposure seems to be stable until June 1997, which suggests that they did not anticipate the crisis. This result goes against commonplaces: if hedge funds did not anticipate the crisis, how could they have triggered it? Of course, this remark is only valid for the funds covered by our analysis and it remains plausible that other funds could have anticipated the crisis. During the first two months of the currency crisis, the mean exposure to the Asian equities dropped by 30 per cent, while the Asian equity market started falling in August 1997.[5] But this reduction does not seem to be permanent, in the sense that the mean exposure reached its pre-crisis level as of October and seemed to become stable again after the crisis.

Caution is needed in interpreting these results. At the aggregated level, hedge funds appear to have changed their strategies only during the first two months of the crisis, which is definitely imprecise. Indeed, why would they have increased their positions in Asian equities while markets were still falling?

An explanation for this is that individual hedge funds reacted differently during the crisis. We can identify two main reactions when an unexpected crisis occurs. First, a manager could close or reduce his exposure following the crisis. In other words, he could behave as a positive feedback trader. The second plausible reaction could be an increase of the market exposure in order to offset losses during the recovery. This strategy is related to the Saint Petersburg paradox.[6] It consists of increasing leverage when the market depletes the fund's capital. Thus, thanks to leverage, losses will be offset during the recovery period. Although this strategy seems to be ideal, it relies on an essential assumption: the fund's leverage must be almost infinite. In the case of limited leverage, the fund may become bankrupt before the recovery period occurs.

We can observe changes in individual Asian hedge funds exposures that occurred during and after the crisis. Six of the 10 funds significantly reduced their exposure during the crisis and generally maintained lower exposures after January 1998. Three funds increased their exposure between June 1997 and September 1998, including two funds that entered this market following the crisis.

These exposures dynamics explain the phenomenon we observed at the aggregated level. We distinguished two distinct behaviours that can be assimilated to positive feedback trading and negative feedback trading (including Saint Petersburg investment). As a consequence, we observed heterogeneous strategy shifts following the crisis, in the sense that their exposure changed significantly in comparison to

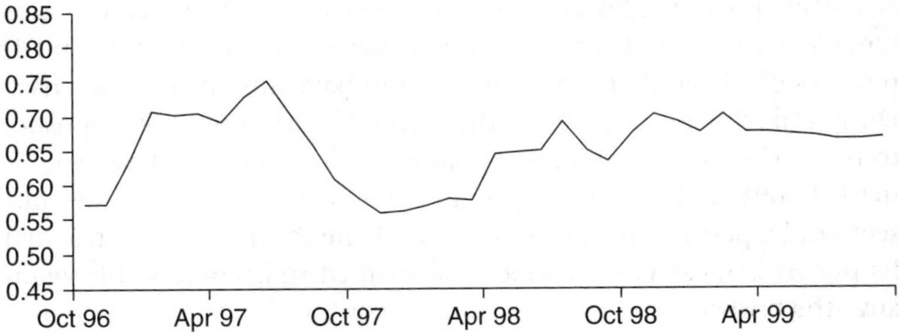

Figure 2.3 Mean estimated exposure to Latin American equities

the pre-crisis period. We also observed a similar result for one fund that took large bets against Asian bonds after the trigger of the crisis, which is equivalent to a change in its strategy as a consequence of the Asian currency devaluations.

As we estimated time varying exposures for all selected factors, we can analyze the impact that the Asian crisis had on the Latin American market and the Eastern European market.

Figure 2.3 represents the mean exposure to the Latin American equity market. This includes exposures of Asian and non-Asian hedge funds to the factor AMLAT. They seem to have decreased Latin American equity positions substantially between June 1997 and January 1998. At the end of the post-crisis period, their exposures nearly reached the pre-crisis level and apparently stabilized themselves after September 1998. We note five Asian hedge funds exposed to the Latin American equity markets. Only two of them reduced their exposures to this market during the crisis, but recovered their initial investment positions at the end of the post-crisis period. Furthermore, the crisis had apparently no impact on the exposures of the three other Asian funds. We then deduce that variations in Asian hedge funds exposures are not sufficient to explain exposure changes at the aggregated level. Thus, non-Asian funds could have changed their strategies during this period. This assumption is confirmed at the individual fund level. Almost one half of the non-Asian funds decreased their exposures to Latin equities during and after June 1997, whereas the other half did not react to this event. In addition, the three funds exposed to the Latin American bond market significantly decreased their positions in this market during and after the crisis.

There may be two different links between the occurrence of a major crisis on a market and the decreases of the positions held in assets of other markets. First, a manager who is exposed to the falling market may need to find liquidities. On the one hand, if he reacts to the crisis by using a strategy based upon the Saint Petersburg paradox, he will have to obtain liquid assets or cash in order to meet the margin requirements that are necessary to increase leverage. On the other hand, he could sell the other illiquid assets (i.e. other emerging market assets) in his portfolio in order to conform to the risk management policy of the fund (which is often linked to simple portfolio trading rules).

Second, a manager who does not hold any asset in the concerned market may make preventive sales on other markets that might be affected by the crisis. This point of view is closely related to the pure contagion theory, in the sense that the considered markets are not necessarily linked by financial channels and are not supposed to be economically dependent upon each other. Thus, such a change in a fund's strategy is solely based upon the manager's anticipations, which may be generated independently from fundamental factors.

We notice similar facts in relation to the Eastern European market, upon which four of the six Asian funds were exposed to the equity factor. Figure 2.4 shows that the mean exposure to the equity factors decreased significantly during the crisis and recovered until default by Russia at the end of the summer in 1998. At the individual fund level, we observe decreases in the exposure to this asset class before and after the crisis. One of these funds, which closed its Asian positions during

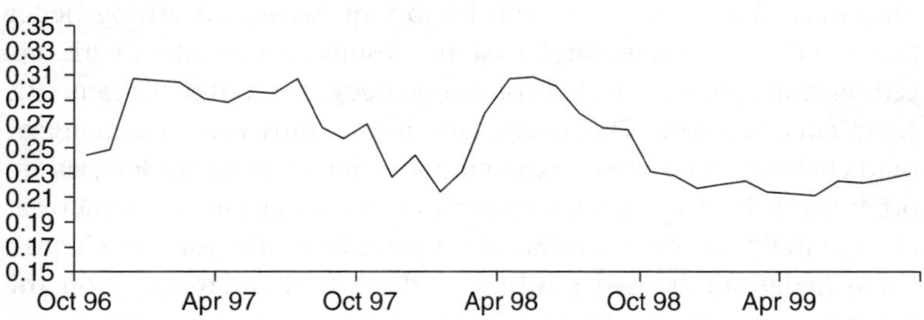

Figure 2.4 Mean estimated exposure to Eastern European equities

the crisis, started investing on the European market at the same time, thus revealing a transfer of his strategy from Asia to Eastern Europe. Similar results are obtained for the Asian funds on the debt market.

No global tendency emerges from our results concerning Asian hedge funds investing on Eastern European markets around the time of the crisis. Three of these funds increased their position, whereas three others decreased theirs. In any event, decreases seem to have been more important, since the mean exposure fell by nearly 30 per cent during this period. The post-crisis changes are much more difficult to interpret because of the proximity of the Russian crisis.

The analysis of the dynamics of emerging markets hedge funds exposures around the Asian currency crisis brought out several points. First, hedge funds strategies have been affected following the crisis, whether in the short or medium term. The strategy shifts that followed the crisis are quite heterogeneous. A major factor is the global disengagement of Asian funds from the Asian market that clearly occurred during the crisis. Most of these funds also modified their exposures to other emerging markets. These changes may have several sources: risk management constraints, liquidity constraints or an increase in the aversion to the Asian market.

Another interesting result is that non-Asian hedge funds reacted to the crisis, particularly on the Latin-American market. A not inconsiderable part of the funds that were exposed to this market decreased their equity exposure. This behaviour can be interpreted as preventive sales generated by the anticipation of a possible contagion phenomenon of Asia towards Latin America.

Conclusion

This work shed light on several important issues concerning hedge funds and markets dynamics. First, our results are consistent with preceding empirical studies that concluded hedge funds did not cause the Asian currency crisis. Due to the fact that we only consider emerging markets hedge funds, we complement other studies that focused on other hedge funds strategies. However, our conclusions are somewhat divergent. Effectively, we produce evidence that, after June 1997, most Asian hedge funds used positive feedback trading strategies on the Asian equity market. This implies that they could have actively contributed to the amplification of the crisis. On the other hand, we show that certain funds (which started to invest in Asian assets after the crisis) used negative feedback trading strategies, thus providing liquidity to the Asian equity market during the crisis. These contrasting results are evidence that hedge funds do not act as a group. We also found that most Asian hedge funds which were holding positions on the Eastern European market before the crisis had a tendency to reduce exposures to this market after June. As their performance and their level of risk were strongly affected by the fall of the Asian markets, they certainly had to limit risky positions (i.e. emerging markets exposure), thus implying decreases in their European exposures.

Second, we extend the analysis of the impact of the Asian crisis to non-Asian funds. Some of them have significantly reduced their exposure to other emerging markets. This behaviour is a way to mitigate the impact that could have been generated by a potential risk transfer of the Asian markets towards other emerging markets. This kind of anticipation is a plausible source of pure contagion. This theoretical concept aims to explain correlated market movements that could occur without a relevant fundamental explanation.

Finally, the fact that hedge funds did not change their investment strategies before the crisis explicitly shows that they had not anticipated it. Furthermore, the heterogeneous changes that occurred in their exposures during and after this event invalidate any assumption about herding behaviour concerning this class of investors. Our conclusions show how tricky it is to define a 'standard hedge fund behaviour'. The heterogeneity of this industry must be taken into account by academics and regulators in future debates.

Appendix

Table 2A Hedge funds exposures

	EM1	EM2	EM3	EM4	EM5	EM6	EM7	EM8	EM9	EM10	EM11	EM12	EM13	EM14	EM15	EM16	EM17	EM18	EM19	EM20	EM21	EM22	EM23	EM24	EM25	EM26
CST	0.00	0.01	−0.01	−0.01*	−0.04**	0.00	0.00	0.00	0.01	0.01	0.00	0.02	−0.01	−0.01**	0.00	0.00	0.00	0.00	0.01*	0.01*	0.04	0.01	0.01	0.01	0.01	0.00
MSCIWI											0.34**		0.69**	−0.37**												
ASIA	−0.23**						0.45**			0.20**	0.11**	0.50**				0.22**	0.22**	0.19*		0.28**		1.01**				
AMLAT		1.01**	0.81**		0.32**	0.87**	0.27**	1.09**	1.10**	0.74**			0.49**			0.36**	0.44**	0.45**			0.73*		1.05**	0.91**	0.22**	
EUREST				0.22**		0.45**	0.24**				0.08**	0.41**			0.32**	0.20**	0.17**			0.19**						0.63**
CAL		1.02**																					1.14**	1.01**		
CEE					−1.10**									−0.54**												
CAS																										
JPMGGBI	−0.89**			−1.15**											−1.34**				−0.45**	−0.66**	−3.05**					
BEE			0.71**	0.50**		0.52**					0.12**	−0.51**		0.37**	0.65**				0.31**		0.56*				0.41**	
BAL						−1.27**								0.95**					0.66**							
BAS							−0.32*			−0.71**																
R^2	0.19	0.88	0.59	0.75	0.31	0.64	0.78	0.61	0.63	0.75	0.81	0.26	0.61	0.89	0.76	0.88	0.92	0.61	0.92	0.50	0.46	0.73	0.85	0.86	0.78	0.36
AR^2	0.16	0.87	0.57	0.73	0.28	0.62	0.76	0.61	0.63	0.74	0.79	0.22	0.60	0.88	0.75	0.87	0.92	0.59	0.92	0.48	0.43	0.72	0.85	0.86	0.77	0.35

Notes: * significant at the 5 per cent level

** significant at the 1 per cent level

Notes

1. They used a rolling regression procedure to estimate hedge funds expoited by the low number of observations used to run the regressions, thus implying high variations of the estimated exposures.
2. The presence of high-water marks implies that if the fund's performance was negative over a period, the manager would have to make good his losses before receiving further incentive fees.
3. Emerging markets equity indices are: MSCI EM Far East, MSCI EM Latin America and MSCI EM Europe (source: www.msci.com). Associated factors are labelled: ASIA, AMLAT and EUREST.

   Emerging markets bond indices are: JP Morgan EMBI+ Asia, JP Morgan EMBI+ Latin America and JP Morgan EMBI+ Europe (source: Datastream). Associated factors are labelled: BAS, BAL, and BEE.

   Developed countries equity and bond indices are: MSCI world index and JP Morgan global government bond index (source: MSCI and Datastream). Associated factors are labelled: MSCIWI and JPMGGBI.

   Currency baskets are constructed as follows: every period, one dollar is invested in each currency. Currencies included in the Asian currency basket are those of the country Assistance Strategy (CAS) of the World Bank.
4. Note that we only consider the 10 funds for which we found significant exposures to ASIA in Figure 2.2.
5. Without wandering away from our problematic, this statement implies that emerging markets hedge funds could have been anticipating (and thus reinforcing) the equity market crash that followed the currency crisis.
6. In probability theory and decision theory the St Petersburg paradox is a paradox that exhibits a random variable whose value is probably very small, and yet has an infinite expected value. This poses a situation where decision theory may superficially appear to recommend a cause of action that no rational person would be willing to take. That appearance evaporates when utilities are taken into account.

References

Brealey, R. and Kaplanis, E. (2001) 'Changes in the Factor Exposures of Hedge Funds', Institute of Finance and Accounting, Working paper (London Business School).

Brown, S.J., Goetzmann, W.N. and Park, J.M. (1998) 'Hedge Funds and the Asian Currency Crisis of 1997', Working paper, Yale University, International Centre for Finance.

Corsetti, G., Dasgupta, A., Morris, S. and Shin, H.S. (2004) 'Does One Soros Make the Difference? A Theory of Currency Crises with Large and Small Traders', *Review of Economic Studies*, 71(1), 87–113.

Eichengreen, B. and Mathieson, D. (1998) 'Hedge Funds and Financial Market Dynamics', Occasional Paper (Washington, DC: IMF).

Eichengreen, B. and Park, B. (2002) 'Hedge Funds Leverage before and after the Crisis', *Journal of Economic Integration*, 17(1), 1–20.

Fung, W. and Hsieh, D. (2000) 'Measuring the Market Impact of Hedge Funds', *Journal of Empirical Finance*, 7, 1–36.

Fung, W., Hsieh, D. and Tsatsaronis, K. (2000) 'Do Hedge Funds Disrupt Emerging Markets?', *Brookings–Wharton Papers on Financial Services*, 2000, 377–421.

Harvey, A.C. (1989) *Forecasting, Structural Time Series Models and the Kalman Filter* (Cambridge, UK: Cambridge University Press).

Monarcha, G. (2004) 'Identifying Hedge Funds Risk Exposures', Working paper (CEFI).

Newbold, P. and Bos, T. (1985) *Stochastic Parameter Regression Models* (Beverly Hills, CA: Sage).

Sharpe, W.F. (1992) 'Asset Allocation: Management Style and Performance Measurement', *Journal of Portfolio Management*, Winter 1992, 7–19.

Swinkels, L. and Van der Sluis, P.J. (2002) 'Return-based Style Analysis with Time-varying Exposures', Discussion paper 96 (Tilburg University, Centre for Economic Research).

3
The Adjustments of Stock Prices to Information on Inflation: Evidence from MENA Countries

Samer A.M. Al-Rjoub

Introduction

An important question that has been asked extensively in the financial economics literature is whether nominal returns contain market assessments of expected and unexpected inflation rates, and whether common stocks are an effective hedge against inflation. However, theoretical attempts to examine the relation between stock returns and inflation diverge. While some studies found a significant negative relationship between unexpected inflation and stock returns (Bodie 1976, Jaffe and Mandelker 1976, Nelson 1976, Fama and Schwert 1977, Fama 1981, Schwert 1981), others found no significant relationship (Pearce and Roley 1985, Hardouvelis 1987, McQueen and Roley 1993). In theses studies, unexpected inflation was created from time series estimation of expected inflation, from the difference between nominal interest rats and inflation, or from experts' predictions.

This chapter extends the empirical evidence by analyzing the reaction of monthly stock returns to the unexpected portion of CPI inflation rate and by capturing the asymmetric shocks to volatility or the news effect of unexpected inflation. This relationship is examined first by using the Nelson and Schwert (1977) first order moving average process to calculate unexpected inflation, and second by using both threshold GARCH (TGARCH) and exponential GARCH (EGARCH) to catch the news effect that unexpected inflation may have on stock returns.

Utilizing a long sample period and a time series measure of expectations and using the threshold ARCH introduced independently by Zakoian (1990) and Glosten, Jagannathan, and Runkle (1993) and the Exponential GARCH model proposed by Nelson (1991), the interaction between the unexpected CPI inflation rate and stock returns is examined. The next section describes the effects of unexpected inflation on stock returns, followed by a presentation of the methodology and description of the data. The EGARCH and TARCH results follow and the chapter closes with a conclusion.

The effects of unexpected inflation

Do nominal returns contain market assessments of expected inflation rates and are common stocks an effective hedge against inflation? Fisher (1930) first elaborated the hypothesis that interest rates contain market forecasts of future inflation rates. Economists thought that this relationship could be easily extended to common stocks and assumed that expected nominal stock returns should adjust uniformly in a one-to-one correspondence with expected inflation.

However, there is little empirical support for the positive inflation–return relationship and the commonly held view that nominal interest rates are reliable predictors of inflation. (Boudloukh and Richardson (1993) document positive long-horizon returns to actual or expected changes in inflation.) Theoretical attempts to examine the relation between stock returns and inflation show that stock returns are actually negatively correlated with expected and unexpected inflation. Indeed, typically, the coefficient of the inflation term in a stock return equation is not only statistically different from 1, but its sign is negative (e.g. Lintner 1975, Bodie 1976, Jaffe and Mandelker 1976, Nelson 1976, and Fama and Schwert 1977, Geske and Roll 1983, Pearce and Roley 1983 and Pearce 1985). This puzzle has been the subject of a great deal of work in the finance literature and several attempts have been made at explaining this puzzle (e.g. Modigliani and Cohn 1979, Feldstein 1980, Fama 1981, Geske and Roll 1983, Titman and Warga 1989).

One of the most widely quoted explanations is offered by the 'money demand proxy hypothesis' proposed by Fama (1981), the collective money illusion proposed by Modigliani and Cohn (1979), and the non-neutralities in the tax treatment of the inventory and depreciation charges proposed by Feldstein (1980). There is also some variance in the hypothesis explaining the relationship between unexpected inflation and stock prices. These variations are based on nominal contracting and tax effects, investors' misperception, and real-activity consequences of unexpected inflation.

Modigliani and Cohn (1979) attribute the negative effect of unexpected inflation to the existence of collective money illusion. Unexpected inflation raises nominal interest rates and if investors use the higher rates to discount future earnings, ignoring the positive effect of inflation on nominal earnings, the results is an incorrect undervaluation of stocks.

Feldstein (1980) argues that inflation lowers stock prices because non-neutralities in the tax treatment of the inventory and depreciation charges cause inflation to lower real after-tax profits. Fama (1981) argues that the negative inflation–stock return relationship is generated by a positive causal link between real output and stock returns coupled with an inverse correlation between real output and inflation. Fama (1981) implicitly argues that unexpected decline in real activity leads to an accommodating rise in inflation created by aggregate supply shocks. The argument in Fama 1981 was extended and further tested in a series of papers: Kaul 1987, Ely and Robinson 1992, Geske and Roll 1983, Balduzzi 1995 and Graham 1996. Kaul (1987) also suggests that, in one way or another, changes in real activity and the money supply is behind the negative relationship between inflation and stock returns. Following the same line, Marshall (1992) argues that the negative inflation–returns correlation may be generated by real economic fluctuations, by monetary fluctuations, or possibly both. Marshall also suggests that this negative correlation is more strongly negative when inflation is caused by fluctuations in real economic activity than when it is caused by monetary fluctuations (supporting Fama's prediction). Geske and Roll (1983) suggest the reverse causality hypothesis between inflation and stock returns; the evidence is still not conclusive. They also suggest that if negative real macroeconomic shocks are accommodated by monetary expansion, we observe a simultaneous decline in stock prices and increase in inflation.

Titman and Warge (1989) offer another explanation where the stock returns are the predictor of inflation using lagged stock returns. This relationship is found to be positive. In a recent contribution,

Hess and Lee (1999) account for the inflation–stock returns relationship with a supply and demand shock. Supply shocks are characterized as shocks to real activity, while the demand shocks originate largely through shocks to the money supply.

Data and methodology

Data

The Emerging Markets Data Base (EMDP) served as our source for information on stock markets in five emerging MENA countries: Bahrain, Egypt, Jordan, Oman, and Saudia Arabia. A stock market index is used to represent the stock markets in each country. For the Consumer Price Index (CPI) data, the International Financial Statistical (IFS) database is used. The inflation rates are calculated as the percentage change in the CPI. All data are monthly. The sample period is different across these countries and can be summarized as follows:

Bahrain	Egypt	Jordan	Oman	Saudia Arabia
1999:01–2002:07	1996:01–2002:07	1978:12–2002:07	1999:01–2002:07	1997:12–2002:07

Methodology

This paper investigates the effect of unexpected inflation on stock returns in five MENA countries: Bahrain, Egypt, Jordan, Oman, and Saudia Arabia using a family of GARCH models. The family nests two basic models: EGARCH[1] in mean and threshold GARCH.

Modelling the asymmetric effect using EGARCH-M and TARCH

Despite the apparent successes of ARCH and GARCH parameterizations, these models cannot capture the asymmetric news effect discovered by Black (1976) and confirmed by Zakoian 1990, Nelson 1991, Engle and Ng 1993, Glosten, Jagannathan, and Runkle 1993, among others. This asymmetric effect (sometimes called the leverage effect) reflects the observed fact that downward movements in the market are followed by higher volatilities than upward movements of the same magnitude. Statistically, the leverage effect occurs when an unexpected drop in price (bad news) increases predictable volatility more than an unexpected increase in price (good news) of similar magnitude. If unexpected inflation is considered bad news for the stock market, then unexpected inflation should be associated with a decrease in stock prices at that time (assuming a one-month lag).

The unexpected inflation–stock return effect is tested using the univariate EGARCH (p, q)-M model as shown below:

i = Baharain, Egypt, Jordan, Oman, and Saudia Arabia

$$R_{it} = \alpha_i + \beta_{im}UNEX + \vartheta\sigma_t^2 + \varepsilon_{it}, \varepsilon_{it} \sim N(0, \sigma_{IT}^2),$$

$$\log(\sigma_{it}^2) = \omega + \delta \cdot \log(\sigma_{it-1}^2) + \aleph \cdot \frac{\varepsilon_{t-1}}{\sqrt{\sigma_{it}^2}} + \gamma\left[\frac{\varepsilon_{t-1}}{\sqrt{\sigma_{it-1}^2}} - \sqrt{2/\pi}\right] \quad (3.1)$$

where

R_{it} is the monthly rate of return on the market portfolio of assets for country i in period t,

UNEX represents the unexpected inflation estimates as the residuals from the first order moving average process of the inflation rate,

σ_{it}^2 is the conditional variance at period t,

ω, δ, $\aleph$, and γ are constant parameters.

In this model, if $\gamma < 0$, then the leverage effect exists and if $\gamma \neq 0$ the impact is asymmetric. The EGARCH model is asymmetric because the level of the standardized errors is included with coefficient γ. This coefficient is typically negative without violating the non-negative variance condition. This allows for positive return shocks to generate less volatility than negative return innovations, all else being equal.

The unexpected inflation–stock return effect is tested using the univariate TARCH (p,q)-M model as shown below:

$$\tilde{R}_{it} = \alpha_i + \beta_{im}UNEX + \vartheta\sigma_t^2 + \varepsilon_{it}, \varepsilon_{it} \sim N(0, \sigma_{IT}^2)$$

$$\sigma_t^2 = \omega + \alpha\varepsilon_{t-1}^2. + \gamma\varepsilon_{t-1}^2 d_{t-1} + \beta\sigma_{t-1}^2 \quad (3.2)$$

where $d_t = 1$ if $\varepsilon_t < 0$, and zero otherwise.

In this model, good news ($\varepsilon_t < 0$) and bad news ($\varepsilon_t > 0$), have differential effects on the conditional variance – good news has an impact of α, while bad news has an impact of $\alpha + \gamma$. If $\gamma > 0$ we say that the leverage effect exists. If $\gamma \neq 0$, the news impact is asymmetric.

Selecting the Wright model to describe the inflation process in MENA countries

An important question arises when we try to describe the inflation process in these five MENA countries: What is the proper model? (i.e. What is the best-fitting ARMA model?). In order to answer this question Ljung–Box Q-statistics is used. If the sample value of Q exceeds the critical value of χ^2 with n degrees of freedom, then at least one of the values of the tested series is statistically different from zero at the specified significance level. In order to test whether the ARMA (p, q) model fits the inflation data, we report the Ljung–Box Q-statistics for the residuals for lags 8 and 12 in Table 3.1.

Table 3.1 shows the results of the best-fitting ARMA models for inflation in Bahrain, Egypt, Jordan, Oman, and Saudia Arabia. Best-fitting ARMA models are determined after constructing the ACF and PACF for the residuals of the estimated model. The Ljung–Box Q-statistics and the serial correlation Lagrange multiplier (LM) tests accept the null hypothesis that there is no serial correlation in the equations. The inflation rate is modelled using an ARMA (1, 1) model and the residuals from inflation regressions represent unexpected inflation.

Table 3.1 Selection of a model using Ljung–Box Q-statistics

	Ljung–Box Q-statistics For AR (1) ARMA (1, 0)	**Ljung–Box Q-statistics for ARMA (1, 1)**
Bahrain	Q(8) LOS* = 0.006 Q(12) LOS = 0.036	Q(8) LOS = 0.173 Q(12) LOS = 0.066
Egypt	Q(8) LOS = 0.819 Q(12) LOS = 0.513	Q(8) LOS = 0.816 Q(12) LOS = 0.517
Jordan	Q(8) LOS = 0.14 Q(12) LOS = 0.02	Q(8) LOS = 0.18 Q(12) LOS = 0.034
Oman	Q(8) LOS = 0.725 Q(12) LOS = 0.114	Q(8) LOS = 0.991 Q(12) LOS = 0.597
Saudia Arabia	Q(8) LOS = 0.876 Q(12) LOS = 0.887	Q(8) LOS = 0.892 Q(12) LOS = 0.910

Note: * Level of significance

EGARCH and TARCH results

The unexpected effects of inflation are investigated simultaneously by incorporating them into two alternative models of monthly returns. Table 3.2 presents the results from the EGARCH-M (p, q), TARCH-M (p, q) models to test for asymmetric effects during the periods of the study. The process is estimated in this step with the method of maximum likelihood using Gauss–Newton BHHH[2] and/or Marquardt methods. The standard errors are computed using the White heteroskedasticity consistent estimator of the covariance matrix (White 1980).

In order to make the point addressed in this study, we report the constant and the slope in the mean equations of EGARCH and TARCH, and the coefficients of the squared residuals and the leverage effect in the variance equations. We test both the news impact and the leverage effect.

EGARCH results in Table 3.2 indicate that unexpected inflation has a negative impact on stock market returns in all the MENA countries. The impact is high and significant in Bahrain, Egypt, Jordan, and Saudia Arabia and significant in Oman. The leverage effect (γ) for Bahrain is negative and statistically different from zero, indicating the existence of the leverage effect in stock market returns during the sample periods. The impact is asymmetric. On the other hand, the leverage effect (γ) for Egypt is positive and statistically different from zero, indicating the non-existence of the leverage effect in stock market returns during the sample period. Results are similar for Jordan. For Oman and Saudia Arabia, there is no news effect of inflation on stock market data.

TARCH results in Table 3.2 show that unexpected inflation has a negative effect on Bahrain (−164.74 with a p-value of (0.00)), Jordanian (−92.28 with a p-value (0.05)), and Saudi stock market returns (−292.2 with a p-value of (0.00)). The coefficients of unexpected inflation are negative and highly significant. Only Oman and Egypt show insignificant results where unexpected inflation shows no effect on stock market return data in the sample period. When testing for the leverage effect, results show the following: (1) γ for Bahrain, Egypt , and Saudi Arabia is negative and significant, indicating that the leverage effect does not exist for these countries, (2) γ is

Table 3.2 News effect of inflation

Coefficients	EGARCH (p,q)−M					TGARCH				
Mean equation	Bahrain	Egypt	Jordan	Oman	Saudi Arbia	Bahrain	Egypt	Jordan	Oman	Saudi Arabia
	1999:01–2002:07	1996:01–2002:07	1978:12–2002:07	1999:01–2002:07	1997:12–2002:07	1999:01–2002:07	1996:01–2002:07	1978:12–2002:07	1999:01–2002:07	1997:12–2002:07
α	29.22	2.12	132.7	93.64	−0.014	7.38	5.31	132.25	96.01	1.58
	(0.02)	(0.00)	(0.00)	(0.00)	(0.00)	(0.00)	(0.00)	(0.00)	(0.00)	(0.03)
β	−60.43	−164.85	−108.47	−278.11	−1.62	−164.74	−1.42	−92.28	268.32	−292.2
	(0.00)	(0.00)	(0.02)	(0.09)	(0.00)	(0.00)	(0.37)	(0.05)	(0.37)	(0.00)
Variance equation										
α						1.65	0.90	0.605	0.955	3.716
						(0.00)	(0.00)	(0.00)	(0.00)	(0.00)
γ	1.15	3.11	0.069	−0.195	−0.246	−3.90	−59.15	−0.059	−0.0053	−5.312
	(0.00)	(0.00)	(0.09)	(0.36)	(0.54)	(0.00)	(0.00)	(0.29)	(0.98)	(0.00)
$\alpha + \gamma$						−2.25	−58.25	0.546	0.9497	−1.596

Notes: This table reports the results of the EGARCH (p,q)-M, and TGARCH (p,q) models. p-values are in parenthesis; α and β are the coefficients for the mean equation in the EARCH-M and the TGARCH; while α and γ are those for the variance equations to represent the leverage affect.

not significantly positive for Jordan and Oman, so there appears to be no asymmetric effect. The results are similar for those of the EGARCHs.

All these results indicate that the stock markets of the listed MENA countries do not feel extreme movements in the markets and, as such, do not experience volatilities. The asymmetric news effect is absent.

To assess the general descriptive validity of the model, a battery of standard specification tests is employed. The test results are presented in Tables 3.3 and 3.4. The adequacy of the specification for the first two conditional moments is verified through serial correlation tests of white noise. We employ the Ljung–Box Q-Test for serial correlation in the squared-standardized residuals (ε_t^2/h_t). All series are free of serial correlation at the standard 1 per cent level of significance. A Jarque–Bera LM test also overwhelmingly rejects the null of normality.

Table 3.3 Diagnostic statistics of the residuals from EGARCH estimation

	EGARCH (p,q) ε_t^2/h_t–squared standardized residuals				ARCH LM test for the GARCH model specification	
	Skewness	**Kurtosis**	**J–B probability**	**Ljung–Box* (24)**	**F-stat**	**P-value**
Bahrain EGARCH (1,1)	15.36	246.13	0.000	1.093	0.00037	0.98
Egypt EGARCH (1,3)	13.79	212.86	0.000	18.525	0008578	0.77
Jordan EGARCH (1,2)	2.56	15.03	0.00	14.694	0.08325	0.77
Oman EGARCH(1,1)	15.36	246.13	0.000	1.093	0.0124	0.911
Saudia Arabia EGARCH (1,3)	7.624	66.00	0.00	23.683	2.22536	0.1369

Notes: This table includes a battery of standard specification tests. The squared standardized residuals (ε_t^2/h) are reported. J–B probability is the p-value for testing for normality in the EGARCH (p,q)-M residuals. Standard errors are computed using the robust inference procedures developed by Bollerslev and Wooldridge (1988).

* The series is free of serial correlation at the standard 1% level of significance.

Table 3.4 Diagnostic statistics of the residuals from TARCH estimation

	EGARCH (p,q) ε_t^2/h_t–squared standardized residuals				ARCH LM test for the GARCH model specification	
	Skewness	**Kurtosis**	**J–B probability**	**Ljung–Box* (24)**	**F-stat**	**P-value**
Bahrain EGARCH (1,1)	14.06	216.79	0.00	14.251	0.506	0.477
Egypt EGARCH (1,2)	16.65	278.7	0.000	0.036	0.0002	0.988
Jordan EGARCH (1,2)	3.145	19.32	0.00	16.44	3.0858	0.80
Oman EGARCH(1,1)	2.17	9.94	0.00	20.284	0.539	0.465
Saudia Arabia EGARCH (1,3)	12.015	171.62	0.00	87.39	2.143	0.144

Notes: This table includes a battery of standard specification tests. The squared standardized residuals (ε_t^2/h) are reported. J–B probability is the p-value for testing for normality in the TARCH (p,q)-M residuals. Standard errors are computed using the robust inference procedures developed by Bollerslev and Wooldridge (1988).
* The series is free of serial correlation at the standard 1% level of significance.

Further, we carry out a Lagrange Multiplier test to examine whether the standardized residuals exhibit additional ARCH. We found that in all cases the variance equations are correctly specified and that there should be no ARCH left in the standardized residuals. The F-test statistics and their P-values indicate this result. All the F-statistics are insignificant across the two sample periods. The coefficients of skewness and kurtosis show severe evidence against the conditional normality assumption in the residuals. The statistics show that returns are negatively skewed, although the skewness statistics are not appreciable. However, all the kurtosis values are much greater than 3, significantly different from that of normal distribution. This indicates that much of the non-normality is due to leptokurtosis. Despite these facts, the estimates are still consistent under quasi-maximum likelihood assumptions. The GARCH models encompass an autocorrelation correction and are robust under non-normality. Overall, results in Table 3.3 and 3.4 support our model specification.

Conclusion

This chapter extends the empirical evidence by analyzing the reaction of monthly stock returns to the unexpected portion of CPI inflation rate, and by capturing the asymmetric shocks to volatility of unexpected inflation in five MENA countries. Both threshold GARCH and exponential GARCH are used to catch the news effect that unexpected inflation may have on stock returns.

After selecting the right model to describe the inflation process in MENA countries, unexpected inflation is regressed over the stock market return for the five MENA countries: Bahrain, Egypt, Jordan, Oman, and Saudia Arabia. Results show a negative and strongly significant relationship between unexpected inflation and stock returns in these countries. Results also indicate that the stock markets of the listed MENA countries do not feel the extreme movements in the markets and, as such, do not experience volatilities. The asymmetric news effect is absent.

Notes

1. For a more detailed specification of EGARCH, see Nelson (1990), and Engle and Ng (1993).
2. The BHHH algorithm follows Newton–Raphson. It replaces the negative of the Hessian by an approximation formed from the sum of the outer product of the gradient vectors for each observation's contribution to the objective function. The Marquardt algorithm modifies the Gauss–Newton algorithm in exactly the same manner as BHHH modifies the Newton–Raphson method. By adding a ridge factor to the Hessian approximation, this correction handles numerical problems when the outer product is near singular, and may improve the convergence rate.

References

Balduzzi, P. (1995) 'Stock Returns and the "Proxy Hypothesis": A New Look at the Data', *Economics Letters*, 48, 47–53.

Black, F. (1976) 'Studies of Stock Price Volatility Changes', in *Proceedings of the 1976 Meetings of the Business and Economic Statistics Section, American Statistical Association*, 177–81.

Bodie, Z. (1976) 'Common Stocks as a Hedge Against Inflation', *Journal of Finance*, 31, 459–70.
Bollerslev, T. and Wooldridge, J.M. (1988) 'Quasi-Maximum, likelihood Estimation of Dynamic Models with Time-Varying Covariances', Working Paper 505, Massachusetts Institute of Technology (MIT), Department of Economics.
Box, G.E.P. and Jenkins, G. (1976) *Time Series Analysis: Forecasting and Control* (New York: Holden-Day).
Boudoukh, J. and Richardson, M. (1993) 'Stock Returns and Inflation: A Long-horizon Perspective', *American Economic Review*, 83, 1346–55.
Ely, D.P. and Robinson, K.J. (1992) 'Stock Returns and Inflation: Future Tests of the Role of the Central Bank', *Journal of Macroeconomics*, 14, 525–43.
Engle, R. and Ng, V. (1993) 'Measuring and Testing the Impact of News on Volatility', *Journal of Finance*, 48, 1749–78.
Fama, E.F. (1981) 'Stock Returns, Real Activity, Inflation and Money', *American Economic Review*, 545–65.
Fama, E. and Schwert, William (1977) 'Asset Return and Inflation', *Journal of Financial Economics*, 5, 115–46.
Fisher, Irving (1930) *The Theory of Interest* (New York: Macmillan).
Feldstein, M. (1980) 'Inflation and the Stock Market', *American Economic Review*, 70, 839–47.
Geske, R. and Roll, R. (1983) 'The Fiscal and Monetary Linkage between Stock Returns and Inflation', *Journal of Finance*, 38, 1–33.
Glosten, L.R., Jagannathan, R. and Runkle, D. (1993) 'On the Relation between the Expected Value and the Volatility of the Normal Excess Return on Stocks', *Journal of Finance*, 48, 1779–801.
Graham, F.C. (1996) 'Inflation, Real Stock Returns and Monetary Policy', *Applied Financial Economics*, 6, 29–35.
Hardouvelis, G. (1987) 'Macroeconomic Information and Stock Prices', *Journal of Economics and Business*, 39,131–40.
Hess, P.J. and Bong-Soo, L. (1999) 'Stock Returns and Inflation with Supply and Demand Disturbances', *Review of Financial Studies*, 12, 1203–18.
Jaffe, J. and Mandelker, G. (1976) 'The "Fisher Effect" for Risky Assets: An Empirical Investigation', *Journal of Finance*, 31, 447–58.
Kaul, G. (1987), 'Stock Returns and Inflation: The Role of the Monetary Sector', *Journal of Financial Economics*, 18, 253–76.
Lintner, J. (1975) 'Inflation and Security Return', *Journal of Finance*, 30, 259–80.
Pearce, D.K. (1985) 'Stock Prices and Economic News', *Journal of Business*, 58, 49–67.
Pearce, D.K. and Roley, V.V. (1983) 'The Reaction of Stock Prices to Unanticipated Changes in Money: A Note', *Journal of Finance*, 38, 1323–33.
McQueen, G. and Roley, V.V. (1993) 'Stock Prices, News, and Business Conditions', *Review of Financial Studies*, 6, 683–707.
Marshall, D.A. (1992) 'Inflation and Asset Returns in a Monetary Economy', *Journal of Finance*, vol. XLVII (4), 1315–42.
Modigliani, F. and Cohn, Richard A. (1979) 'Inflation, Rational Valuation and the Market', *Financial Analysts Journal*, March/April, 24–44.

Nelson, C.R. (1976) 'Inflation and Rates of Return on Common Stock', *Journal of Finance*, 31, 471–83.

Nelson C.R. and Schwert, G.W. (1977) 'Short-term Interest Rates as Predictors of Inflation: On Testing the Hypothesis that the Real Rate of Interest is Constant', *American Economic Review*, 67, 478–86.

Nelson, D.B. (1990) 'Stationarity and Persistence in the GARCH (1,1) Model', *Economic Theory*, 6, 318–34.

Nelson, D.B. (1991) 'Conditional Heteroskedasticity in Asset Returns: A New Approach', *Econometrica*, 59, 347–70.

Schwert, G.W. (1981) 'The Adjustment of Stock Prices to Inflation', *Journal of Finance*, 36, 15–29.

Titman, S. and Warga, A. (1989) 'Asset Pricing and Expected Inflation', *Journal of Finance* 41, 209–23.

White, H. (1980) 'A Heteroskedasticity-Consistent Covarience Matrix and a Direct Test for Heteroskedasticity', *Econometrica*, 48, 817–38.

Zakoian, J.M. (1990) 'Threshold Heteroskedastic Models', Manuscript (Paris: CREST, INSEE).

4

Portfolio Management and Financial Market Integration of Emerging MENA Stock Markets

*Simon Neaime**

Introduction

Over the last decade, world stock markets have become highly integrated due to the cross-listing of stocks, improved capital market efficiency – as a result of reductions in the cost of information – and the removal of barriers to the flow of international financial capital. The finance literature[1] originally focused on the more mature stock markets and their prospects of enhancing and diversifying international portfolios (see, for example, Arshanapalli and Doukas 1993, and Eun and Shim 1989). These studies, which focused on the US and European stock markets, argued that the US market and, to some extent, the UK and French stock markets are already integrated and thus cannot offer potential for diversification to international investors.

Recently, however, there has been a shift in focus in order to study the emerging and less mature financial markets (see, for example, Darrat and Hakim 1997, Neaime and Hakim 2002, Hakim and Neaime 2003, and Neaime 2006). This recent shift is due to the fact that these emerging and smaller markets may offer potential for diversification to international portfolios that is not available in other more developed markets. However, this new literature is still fairly limited, and has focused on the issue of stock market efficiency, as well as on the integration of these markets with international and regional markets. Al-Loghani (1995) and Gandhi, Saunders, and

Woodward (1980) studied the Kuwait stock market and tried to measure its informational efficiency. Their empirical findings point to the inefficiency of that market. Butler and Malaikah (1992) added Saudi Arabia to their analysis and again found that both markets are informationally inefficient. Other studies covered shorter periods of time, and did not touch on the issue of portfolio diversification. These include El-Erian and Kumar (1995), which covered five markets over the period 1992–94, and Darrat and Hakim (1997), covering three markets and the period 1996–97.

It is, however, well known that as emerging markets mature, they are likely to become increasingly sensitive to the volatility of stock markets elsewhere. Their increasing degree of integration with world markets will diminish their ability to enhance and diversify international portfolios, and will make them more vulnerable to world financial disturbances. Also, rapid movements in short-term portfolio capital when stock markets are open to foreign investors and capital transfers uncontrolled may increase the vulnerability of MENA's developing market economies to the financial liberalizing effects of globalization. Such integration and liberalization of financial markets in East Asia – notably Thailand and South Korea in 1996–97 – had serious effects as portfolio capital was quickly liquidated, leading to a major financial collapse in both banking and industry. Yet in some countries, such as Saudi Arabia and Oman, foreign investors are not allowed to invest at will, and this helps to reduce volatility in those two stock markets, while at the same time reducing their effectiveness in mobilizing external (non-Saudi or Omani) financial resources. That is, there is a price to pay in adopting either an open financial market or a restricted one. The issue for countries of the MENA region is one of choice and trade-off.

Given these developments among the MENA Gulf Cooperation Council (GCC) stock markets, it is pertinent to ask if shocks in one market should affect other markets. Countries that share geographical proximity and have similar groups of investors are more than likely to have markets that influence each other. And when a stock is dually listed in two countries, shocks in one market can be easily transmitted to the other market through spillover and contagion effects. In addition, investors in one market may react in a similar fashion directly and indirectly to an initial shock in another market.

In this chapter, we focus on the linkages between the Middle East and North Africa (MENA) stock markets on the one hand, and the linkages between MENA markets and the more mature markets of the USA, UK, and French stock markets, on the other. We first examine stock market efficiency among the stock markets of Bahrain, Kuwait, Saudi Arabia, Egypt and Jordan during the period 1994–2002. Next, we investigate the long-run dynamic interactions between these stock markets to study whether the MENA markets are regionally and/or internationally integrated by applying Johansen cointegration techniques, as this will have an important bearing on the potential for diversification that these markets can offer to international investors. The short-run dynamic interactions between these stock markets will also be examined by applying Granger causality tests to study the directional effects that each market has on the other.

The next section of this chapter highlights the recent developments in MENA stock markets. We then outline the empirical methodology and present the empirical results. Finally, the chapter closes with our conclusions and our observations on policy implications.

MENA stock markets developments: 1994–2002

Capital markets in the MENA region have traditionally been less important in channeling financial funds. A fairly developed commercial banking system has taken the lead in attracting and distributing funds. With the possible exception of Kuwait and Jordan, MENA equity markets have only come to the fore since the 1990s. Despite their small market capitalization, in recent years MENA equity markets have exhibited performance characteristics parallel to other emerging markets in similar stages of development.

Despite the poor performance of MENA stock markets over the past two decades, there have been some encouraging recent indicators pointing to the repatriation of MENA capital back to the region. In addition, MENA stock markets have recently emerged as good examples of newly emerging capital markets, with significant growth potential. These markets have become of interest to world investors and policy makers, due to the significant flow of funds into these emerging financial markets, especially after the financial crisis in East Asia (1997–98), the Argentinean crisis (2001), and the events of

September 11 in the USA. Consequently, the stock markets of Egypt and Jordan have become leading capital markets in the MENA region, with relatively rising significance.[2]

Moreover, the MENA GCC countries have been devoting considerable efforts to integrating their capital markets. The GCC region appears to be challenged by this mobilization and is devoting more attention to improving the operation of domestic financial markets. In doing so, significant strides have been made toward the development of proper legal and regulatory systems. Efforts are also being devoted towards full monetary integration through the adoption of a common currency by 2010. On the other hand, GCC capital markets are also expected to benefit from the repatriation of Saudi capital from investments in the US stock market. This is due to recent fears of ad hoc freezing of Saudi deposits in US banks justified by measures taken by the US authorities to freeze assets in its 'war against terrorism'. In addition, the recent hike in oil prices to around US$ 50/barrel (Texas Crude Prices), has significantly affected stock market capitalization in the GCC countries in the short-run by increasing their equity price volatility. That is, should oil prices decline again, the observed buoyancy in the stock markets of the region may subside as portfolio capital may then exit elsewhere.

In addition, foreign investors have recently acquired better access to the GCC stock markets and are exempt from paying withholding taxes, with free repatriation of capital and dividends. Saudi Arabia and Kuwait have been taking considerable measures to further open up their capital markets to foreign investors. For example, until relatively recently, only nationals from Kuwait and GCC states had been allowed to trade directly on the Kuwaiti Stock Exchange, although foreign residents could participate through mutual funds. In May of 2000, Kuwait approved regulations governing non-Gulf Arab investment in Kuwaiti shares in a move to boost the country's sagging bourse, and allow foreigners from non-Gulf Arab states to buy shares of local companies. In Saudi Arabia, reform measures were announced in the second half of the year 2000, in particular, non-Saudis could only invest in local shares through established mutual funds.

In Table 4.1, we include three quantitative measures of stock market development: the number of companies listed on domestic stock markets, stock market capitalization, and the number of shares traded. We hypothesize that as stock market development increases, so does economic growth. Stock markets have two general functions. First, they allow corporations to raise capital externally. Corporations must meet certain criteria set by the market to raise capital successfully. By going to the external market to raise funds, a process of certification is initiated and the corporation's project is evaluated. The issuance of securities, therefore, requires some investigation of the corporation's existing financial situation, profitability and management policies. The performance of the firm, and especially of its managers, is therefore monitored to ensure that resources within the firm are allocated and used efficiently. Even after the capital is raised, the scrutiny continues, with approval or disapproval reflected in stock prices. Stock markets thus impose a discipline on firms and their managers.

The second major function of stock markets is their liquidity. Few transactions on the stock market directly involve the corporation that issued the shares. Transactions take place between two anonymous investors. One attractive feature of investing in stocks in well developed markets is their liquidity: investors can easily buy and sell their shares in a corporation. We use the number of traded shares as an indicator of liquidity in the stock market. We argue that as liquidity increases, the cost of entering and exiting the stock market (transaction costs) falls, thus stimulating further investments. We use stock market capitalization and the number of companies listed on stock markets to capture these effects. The number of companies listed provides a measure of the number of firms that have met the standards of the market, but does not indicate the amount of capital raised.

Table 4.1 indicates that MENA's capital markets are showing positive performances in recent years, particularly in terms of growth, liquidity and transparency. More portfolio investment is being channeled to the region and markets are heading towards more openness. However, much more can be done to reach full liberalization, especially in the GCC–MENA economies. Among the GCC countries, only Bahrain's financial market is fully accessible to foreigners; others allow non-residents to own shares but only through mutual funds. The Egyptian and Jordanian economies do not have any restrictions regarding the access of foreign investors.

Egypt's market capitalization experienced a considerable growth improvement amounting to 518 per cent between 1994–2002, with the number of listed companies increasing by 64 per cent and the

Table 4.1 Measures of stock market developments, 1994–2002

	Date	Number of companies listed		Stock market capitalization (US$ billion)		Growth 1994–02	Volume traded (millions)	
		1994[1]	2002	1994[2]	2002	(%)	1994[3]	2002
Egypt	1950	700	1150	4.258	26.338	518.45	27.27	832.8
Kuwait	1952	48	95	10.967	35.098	220.03	2519.16	42163.2
Saudi Arabia	1935	62	68	38.693	74.851	93.45	152.10	1735.8
Bahrain	1957	34	40	5.129	7.716	50.44	257.10	352.9
Oman	1989	68	140	1.856	5.27	183.82	42.10	191.1
Jordan	1978	95	158	4.626	7.087	53.18	133.82	455.7

Notes:

[1] Number of companies listed is the year-end totals, excluding listed investment funds where possible.
[2] Stock market capitalization: year-end total value traded of listed domestic company shares.
[3] Volume traded: year-end total market values of listed domestic companies.

Source: Arab Monetary Fund

number of traded shares reaching 832.86 million. This can be explained by the introduction of Egypt's economic policy reforms, the market's responsiveness to the government's accelerated privatization programme, the increasing interest of foreign institutions in the Egyptian market and the enhanced performance of Egyptian companies reflected in increased profits.

The number of listed companies on Kuwait's stock exchange reached 95 in 2002, a two-fold increase since 1994. Market capitalization increased from US$ 10.96 to 35.09 billion, reflecting a 220 per cent growth rate, and the number of traded shares increased significantly from 2519 to 42163 million. The Kuwaiti market is fully accessible to all GCC nationals, however; restrictions on foreigners are still relatively high. Saudi Arabia's stock market activity managed to record a growth of 93.45 per cent between 1994 and 2002, with the number of traded shares rising by 1583.74 million. While market capitalization experienced a noticeable improvement, the number of listed companies hardly increased – 62 companies in 1994 to 68 companies in 2002. Bahrain's capital market performance is improving; nevertheless, it is still not yet fully developed. Market capitalization exhibits a growth of 50.44 per cent during the period under study, and the number of traded shares increased by 100 million. The number of listed companies on the Omani stock exchange rose from 68 in 1994 to 140 in 2002. Market capitalization jumped from US$ 1856 to 5268 million, recording a 183 per cent growth rate, and the number of traded shares more than doubled, reaching 191.11 million in 2002. The Jordanian market performance is similar to the Bahraini stock market. After expanding by 53 per cent relative to 1994, market capitalization stood at US$ 7.087 billion in 2002. The number of listed companies increased by 66 per cent and the number of traded shares jumped from 133.82 million in 1994 to 455.72 million in 2002.

Most of MENA's financial markets are still partially or fully inaccessible to foreign investors. The ease with which capital flew into South East Asia is absent in the MENA region. This might not be a negative factor after all, as some financial researchers have argued. The limited share of foreign participation has been a boon for the MENA stock markets during the South East Asian crisis in October 1997. The small reliance on foreign funds helped insulate MENA's markets from the severe repercussions felt in other emerging markets that were more dependent on foreign capital.

Many analysts believe that the rapid and substantial growth in East Asia was due to the fast liberalization of these financial markets, a factor that contributed to the fast transmission of the crisis from one company to another and from one financial system to another. Even though growth rates in the MENA region appear to be much lower than their emerging markets counterparts, their segmentation from the rest of the world has contributed to their isolation from foreign financial shocks. While financial liberalization might be important for sustained growth, fast liberalization might however become destructive to growth.

Empirical methodology and results

Data and descriptive statistics

In the empirical section of the chapter, we use weekly closing price series for the stock markets of a selected MENA sample consisting of Bahrain, Kuwait, Saudi Arabia, Jordan, and Egypt. Oman is excluded from the empirical analysis due to lack of data series. Our sample spans the period 1994–2002. Compounded week-to-week returns are

Table 4.2 Descriptive statistics for market returns, 1994–2002

	USA	UK	Paris	Egypt	Jordan	Kuwait	Saudi Arabia	Bahrain
Mean (%)	0.4	0.35	0.29	0.18	0.17	0.43	0.43	0.71
Median (%)	0.61	0.58	0.45	−0.53	−0.54	0.19	0.17	0.69
Maximum (%)	3.69	3.69	3.01	9.63	5.61	4.78	7.65	5.63
Minimum (%)	−4.42	−5.02	−5.23	−5.54	−3.65	−5.49	−5.16	−4.89
Standard deviation (%)	1.53	1.24	1.21	3.30	1.60	1.35	1.43	1.88
Skewness	−62.3	−59.8	−63.5	115.36	51.36	24.98	149.43	7.01
Kurtosis	5.20	4.89	4.01	3.58	3.65	5.36	9.56	4.62
Jarque–Bera	17.4	22.6	18.5	42.78	8.61	163.2	263.1	1.65
probability	0	0	0	0	0.01	0	0	0.46
No. of weeks	468	468	468	468	468	468	468	468

calculated as the natural log differences in prices: ln (P_t/P_{t-1}). We also introduce the more mature stock markets of the USA, UK, and Paris. Table 4.2 presents some selected descriptive statistics. It is clear that the highest weekly return is observed for Bahrain, while the smallest belongs to Jordan. In terms of risks, Egypt has the highest standard deviation, followed by Bahrain and Jordan. The highest negative skewdness belongs to the more mature markets of the USA, UK, and Paris. In terms of normality, as indicated by the Jarque–Bera statistic, most of the MENA stock returns seem to depart from normality. The same is also true for the more mature markets.

Market efficiency of MENA stock markets

In this section, we use weekly closing price series to study whether MENA stock markets are efficient in allocating information and funds to productive investments – stock market efficiency implies higher growth rates. The next section studies stock market integration of the MENA markets and explores whether these markets are regionally/internationally integrated.

To address the question of market efficiency, we analyze the stochastic nature of MENA's stock market prices by testing for unit roots. This approach is useful to test for departures from the random walk hypothesis, and whether stock market returns distribution in the MENA region deviate from normality. These findings contribute to a more comprehensive understanding of the nature of the return generating process in the MENA countries. To that end, we model each series according to the following process:

$$y_t = \beta_0 + \beta_1 t + \alpha y_{t-1} + u_t, \quad (4.1)$$

where β_0 is a drift parameter, and t is a time trend. We test for unit roots using Phillips and Perron (1988). Essentially, the test is the hypothesis $\gamma = 1$ in the following equation:

$$\Delta P_t = \lambda_0 + \lambda_1 t + \gamma P_{t-1} + \zeta_t. \quad (4.2)$$

The results of the unit root tests are provided in Table 4.3. The Phillips–Perron test results indicate that the MENA markets are non-stationary in the levels. However, Saudi Arabia's case is unique because of the limited liquidity of that market. However, unit roots in the first differences of the stock prices are rejected at the 1 per cent significance level, suggesting that returns (or stock price changes) are stationary. We conclude that, with the exception of Saudi Arabia, weekly stock prices in the MENA region are integrated in the order of 1: I(1), and therefore can be modelled as random walk processes. This finding also substantiates that the MENA stock prices are weak form efficient. A semi-strong or strong form efficient financial market helps reduce information costs, overcome problems of asymmetric information, improve resource allocation and enhance growth by ensuring that capital is allocated to projects with the potentially highest returns. MENA financial markets still need to be more transparent. The disclosure of financial information is still weak, and sometimes totally absent. This is one of the reasons why, until now,

Table 4.3 Market efficiency tests

	Bahrain	Egypt	Jordan	Kuwait	Saudi Arabia
PP Prices in levels	−0.99	−0.56	−1.03	0.7	−4.23
PP First differences	−7.89	−5.63	−8.03	−5.68	–

Notes:
[1] PP is the Phillips and Perron unit root test.
[2] Critical values: −3.64 (1 per cent); −2.89 (5 per cent); −2.62 (10 per cent).

MENA stock markets have been unable to channel funds properly and fully to productive investments. The MENA banking system is still the major source of funds for many MENA projects undertaken.

Cointegration tests

Given the evidence on the unit roots, we next examine whether the series are cointegrated. According to Engle and Granger (1987), two or more variables are said to be cointegrated if each variable individually is integrated in the order of one (say) but a linear combination of the variables is integrated of a lower order (say zero).

The statistical concept of cointegration is a useful device to formalize financial convergence, and evaluate empirically the prospects of regional and international financial integration. If there exists stationary linear combinations of a set of n non-stationary variables, then we say that these variables are cointegrated. These linear combinations or cointegration relations describe stable long-run equilibria among these variables that are driven by a number of common stochastic trends. If the number of cointegrating relations is r, then the number of common stochastic trends is $n - r$. For a concrete example, consider the stock return series of Egypt and Jordan and Saudi Arabia, and assume that each is a non-stationary variable. If the three returns series are cointegrated once, then they are bound together by a stable long-run equilibrium relation, which in turn implies that the stock markets of the three countries have converged to two stochastic common trends that determine the stable equilibrium relation. The conclusion would then be that the three stock markets are financially integrated. For the interpretation of the empirical results, there will be complete financial integration among a set of n stock markets, if there exist $r = n - 1$ cointegrating relations, and a single common stochastic trend among them. Otherwise, if r is in the interval $0 < r < \mathrm{n} - 1$, then there will be only partial integration of stock markets. Convergence in this context means that stock returns move in a coordinated manner, so that the variables of interest move to long-run equilibrium, and do not drift too far apart over time. We comment on these issues further in the context of the analysis of the empirical results.

The null hypothesis of no cointegration is tested against the alternative hypothesis of cointegration. A large negative test statistic is consistent with the hypothesis of cointegration. The Johansen cointegration tests report no evidence against the null hypothesis of no cointegration among the GCC stock markets. There appears to be strong convergence among the stock returns of the stock markets of Saudi Arabia, Kuwait and Bahrain. Table 4.4 reports the existence of two cointegrating vectors and one stochastic trend, indicating full financial integration between the GCC stock markets.[3] This result is not surprising, since GCC countries have devoted significant efforts to the integration of their financial and monetary policies, and have removed all the barriers to the flow of capital. This is, however, not the case when one includes the remaining non-GCC MENA stock markets of Jordan and Egypt. Table 4.5 reports the existence of no

Table 4.4 Cointegration tests, MENA–GCC stock markets[1,2]

Hypothesis Null[3]	Alternative	Test statistics	Critical values[4] (5%)	Critical values[4] (1%)
$r = 0$	$r \geq 1$	36.54**	29.68	35.65
$r \leq 1$	$r \geq 2$	17.56*	15.41	20.04
$r \leq 2$	$r = 3$	0.35	3.76	6.65

Notes:
[1] The Johansen cointegration likelihood ratio test is based on the trace of the stochastic matrix.
[2] The test allows for a linear deterministic trend in the data.
[3] r represents the number of cointegrating vectors. Maximum lag 4 years in VAR.
[4] **and * indicate significance at the 1 per cent and 5 per cent levels of significance respectively. The asymptotic critical values are from Osterwald–Lenum (1992).

Table 4.5 Cointegration tests, MENA stock markets[1,2]

Hypothesis Null[3]	Alternative	Test statistics	Critical values[4] (5%)	Critical values[4] (1%)
$r = 0$	$r \geq 1$	86.23	94.15	103.18
$r \leq 1$	$r \geq 2$	55.89	68.52	76.07
$r \leq 2$	$r \geq 3$	39.65	47.21	54.46
$r \leq 3$	$r \geq 4$	22.45	29.68	35.65
$r \leq 4$	$r = 5$	4.55	15.41	20.04

Notes:
[1] The Johansen cointegration likelihood ratio test is based on the trace of the stochastic matrix.
[2] The test allows for a linear deterministic trend in the data.
[3] r represents the number of cointegrating vectors. Maximum lag 4 years in VAR.
[4] The asymptotic critical values are from Osterwald–Lenum (1992).

Table 4.6 Cointegration tests, GCC stock markets and world markets[1,2]

Hypothesis Null[3]	Alternative	Test statistics	Critical values[4] (5%)	(1%)
$r = 0$	$r \geq 1$	92.53	95.06	102.12
$r \leq 1$	$r \geq 2$	61.96	69.43	77.01
$r \leq 2$	$r \geq 3$	40.75	47.01	55.12
$r \leq 3$	$r \geq 4$	23.03	30.48	36.85
$r \leq 4$	$r \geq 5$	10.25	15.41	20.04
$r \leq 5$	$r = 6$	1.53	3.76	6.65

Notes:
1 The Johansen cointegration likelihood ratio test is based on the trace of the stochastic matrix.
2 The test allows for a linear deterministic trend in the data.
3 r represents the number of cointegrating vectors. Maximum lag 4 years in VAR.
4 The asymptotic critical values are from Osterwald–Lenum (1992).

cointegrating vector among the five MENA markets. It also reports the existence of five stochastic trends. Thus, there is no convergence in the stock returns of the MENA stock markets, and stock returns move independently of each other.

To further explore the international financial integration of the MENA stock markets, we next introduce the three more mature markets of the USA, UK, and Paris. Again Table 4.6 indicates that the GCC markets of Saudi Arabia, Kuwait and Bahrain appear to be segregated from the world financial markets. This means that the GCC rich stock markets are in a position to offer potential for diversification to international investors. However, this is not the case when we consider the remaining stock markets of Egypt and Jordan and the more mature markets. Table 4.7 points to the existence of three cointegrating vectors and two stochastic trends. The existence of two stochastic trends indicates that the returns in two out of the remaining five stock markets move independently. Therefore, one can safely conclude that the stock markets of Egypt and Jordan have matured and they appear to be financially integrated with the world stock markets.

Regional financial integration of MENA stock markets

This section performs Granger causality tests to examine the relationship between MENA stock market returns. Weekly data of stock returns are used to investigate the effects of unidirectional and Bi-directional causality.

Table 4.7 Cointegration tests, non-GCC MENA stock markets and world markets[1,2]

Hypothesis Null[3]	Alternative	Test statistics	Critical values[4] (5%)	(1%)
$r = 0$	$r \geq 1$	110.25**	95.06	102.12
$r \leq 1$	$r \geq 2$	77.52**	69.43	77.01
$r \leq 2$	$r \geq 3$	48.21*	47.01	55.12
$r \leq 3$	$r \geq 4$	23.03	30.48	36.85
$r \leq 4$	$r = 5$	10.25	14.23	21.84

Notes:
[1] The Johansen cointegration likelihood ratio test is based on the trace of the stochastic matrix.
[2] The test allows for a linear deterministic trend in the data.
[3] *r* represents the number of cointegrating vectors. Maximum lag 6 years in VAR.
[4] ** and * indicate significance at the 1 per cent and 5 per cent levels of significance respectively. The asymptotic critical values are from Osterwald–Lenum (1992).

The causality tests are conducted for two lags. Formally, let Y and X represent two series, Granger causality addresses the question as to whether X is linearly informative about a future Y. This would hold true only when event X precedes event Y; this presumes that the current and past observations of X help in the forecast of Y. To conduct the test, each series is represented as a vector autoregression and regressed on its lag and those of other variables. The empirical results are presented in Table 4.8. With regard to inter-MENA linkages, we find Cairo playing a somewhat dominant role. This is surprising, since the size and liquidity of the Saudi market dwarfs the characteristics of Cairo's. Specifically, Egypt seems to impact Bahrain, Jordan, Kuwait and Saudi Arabia. Saudi Arabia plays a somewhat less dominant role but appears to impact the remaining MENA markets. We fail to discern any link between Jordan on the one hand and Cairo, Bahrain and Kuwait on the other. Overall, the inter-MENA linkages are relatively weak, indicating little regional financial integration and significant differences existing among these markets.

The East Asian stock markets were already highly regionally and internationally integrated before the 1997 crisis. Investors in one country had full access to any other Asian stock market. Almost all of

Table 4.8 Summary of pairwise Granger causality patterns

Null Hypothesis **Y has no impact on X** **X has no impact on Y**	**F-Stat.**	**Prob.**
E does not cause J	2.18	0.12
J does not cause E	0.44	0.64
E does not cause B	3.22	0.05
B does not cause E	0.05	0.94
E does not cause K	5.94	0.006
K does not cause E	1.30	0.28
E does not cause SA	5.42	0.009
SA does not cause E	0.71	0.49
SA does not cause K	4.56	0.018
K does not cause SA	0.01	0.99
SA does not cause B	3.26	0.051
B does not cause SA	0.10	0.90
J does not cause B	0.05	0.94
B does not cause J	0.44	0.64
J does not cause K	0.05	0.94
K does not cause J	0.23	0.79

Note: Pairwise Granger causality tests are conducted for 4 lags.

these stock markets had cross listings of stocks between them. That is, any investor is able to trade on any of the East Asian stock markets. After the financial crisis erupted in Korea, the crisis transmitted rapidly to other stock markets and regional integration turned out to be an efficient conduit for the swift transmission of financial shocks from one stock market to another.

In summary, our results confirm a belief that the MENA region is maturing and on the verge of becoming the next 'emerging region'. Our results also cast doubt on the extent to which the MENA markets are regionally integrated. Although this is hindering the intra-regional flow of capital and growth in the MENA region, however, in the case of a crisis erupting in one of the region's financial market, its effects might be dampened quickly and financial losses minimized. On the contrary in East Asia, the fast transmission of the crisis resulted in huge financial losses and financial assets became available at fire sale prices across East Asia.

Conclusion

This chapter has highlighted the main features and characteristics of the MENA stock markets over the last decade. It was shown that the MENA stock markets are showing growth and performance characteristics similar to other emerging markets worldwide. The MENA region also appears to be benefiting from the recent hikes in oil prices, and from financial crises occurring in other developing countries. In addition, the relative closeness of some financial markets in the region seems to have protected those markets from the backlashes of the recent financial and currency crises.

The empirical results have shown that the MENA financial markets are still inefficient in channeling funds to appropriate investment. This seems to be translating into lower growth performances, despite the evidence of weak form market efficiency for some of the markets. Moreover, this chapter has also shown that the stock markets of Jordan and Egypt have already matured and are fully accessible to foreign investors. This has rendered these markets unable to offer potential for diversification to international portfolio managers. This is, however, not the case for the remaining MENA markets of Saudi Arabia, Kuwait, and Bahrain. While these markets are relatively closed, they are still able to offer regional and international potential for diversification, mainly through mutual funds.

The removal of the restrictions and barriers to the flow of capital into MENA financial markets is expected to improve and enhance economic growth and development in these countries. The finance literature has shown that there exists a strong link between financial liberalization and economic growth. Increased inter-MENA liberalization will not only increase allocative efficiency within MENA, as the experience of the developed economies shows, but will also provide MENA investors with greater opportunities to diversify their portfolios and reduce risks. Increased financial liberalization within MENA is expected to enhance regional intermediation of resources through close integration of financial markets and increased access of MENA residents to finance investment in the region's financial markets. In addition, MENA investors will have access to a variety of risks adjusted rates of return to enhance the efficiency of portfolio allocation and diversification, which will foster the efficiency of MENAs' financial markets. Increased liberalization within the MENA region is expected to attract important portfolio and direct investments to the area.

Notes

* Financial support from the University Research Board of the American University of Beirut is greatly acknowledged. The author is also grateful to two anonymous referees for valuable comments and suggestions on an earlier draft.

1. For extensive coverage of the finance literature on the international financial integration of the US and European stock markets, see also Campbell and Hamao (1992), Kasa (1992), Malkamäki (1992), Engle and Susmel (1993), Park and Fatemi (1993), and Gjerde and Sættem (1995).
2. According to World Bank World Development Indicators (2003), and from a mere zero foreign portfolio capital inflows into equities to Egypt prior to 1997, the figure is at US$ 4 billion following the Asian crisis. The figures are almost the same for Jordan. Prior to 1997, there were no portfolio equity flows into Jordan; however, post-1997 the figure jumps to about US$ 327 million.
3. The presence of one stochastic trend indicates that one of the stock market return moves independently of the other two.

References

Al-Loughani, N.E. (1995) 'Random Walk in Thinly-Traded Stock Markets: The Case of Kuwait', *Arab Journal of Administrative Sciences*, 3, 189–209.

Arshanapalli, B. and Doukas, J. (1993) 'International Stock Market Linkages: Evidence from the Pre- and Post-October 1987 Period', *Journal of Banking and Finance*, 17, 193–208.

Butler, K.C. and Malaikah, S.J. (1992) 'Efficiency and Inefficiency in Thinly Traded Stock Markets: Kuwait and Saudi Arabia', *Journal of Banking and Finance*, 16, 197–210.

Campbell, J.Y. and Hamao, Y. (1992) 'Predictable Returns in the United States and Japan: A Study of Long Term Capital Markets Integration', *Journal of Finance*, 47, 43–70.

Darat, A. and Hakim, S. (1997) 'Price Linkages, Efficiency, and Integration of Emerging Stock Markets in the Middle East', Paper presented at Conference on Regional Trade, Finance and Labor Markets in Transition. Beirut, 7–9 October.

El Erian, M. and Kumar, M. (1995) 'Emerging Equity Markets in Middle Eastern Countries', in *Development of Financial Markets in the Arab Countries, Iran and Turkey,* Cairo: Economic Research Forum for the Arab Countries, Iran and Turkey, 129–75.

Engle, R. and Granger, C.W.J. (1987) 'Co-integration and Error Correction: Representation, Estimation and Testing, *Econometrica'*, 55, 251–76.

Engle, R.F. and Susmel, R. (1993) 'Common Volatility in Informational Equity Markets', *Journal of Business Economics and Statistics*, 11, 167–76.
Eun, C. and Shim, S. (1989) 'International Transmission of Stock Market Movements', *Journal of Financial and Quantitative Analysis*, 24, 241–56.
Gandhi, D.K., Saunders, A. and Woodward, R.S. (1980) 'Thin Capital Markets: A Case Study of the Kuwaiti Stock Market', *Applied Economics*, 12, 341–9.
Gjerde, O. and Sættem, F. (1995) 'Linkages among European and World Stock Markets', *European Journal of Finance*, 1, 165–79.
Granger, Clive W.J. (1969) 'Investing Causal Relations by Econometric Models and Cross-Spectral Methods', *Econometrica*, 37, 424–38.
Hakim, S. and Neaime, S. (2003) 'Mean-Reversion across MENA Stock Markets: Implications for Derivative Pricing', *International Journal of Business*, 8(3), 348–58.
Kasa, K. (1992) 'Common Stochastic Trends in International Stock Markets', *Journal of Monetary Economics*, 29, 95–124.
Malkamäki, M. (1992) 'Cointegration and Causality of Stock Markets in Two Small Open Economies and their Major Trading Partner Nations', Bank of Finland Research Department Discussion paper 16/92.
Neaime, S. (2006) 'Portfolio Diversification and Correlations in Returns and Volatilities in Emerging MENA Stock Markets', *Thunderbird International Business Review*.
Neaime, S. and Hakim, S. (2002) 'Price Linkages and Integration of MENA Stock Markets', *International Review of Comparative Public Policy*, 13, 63–86.
Osterwald-Lenum, M. (1992) 'A Note with Quantiles of the Asymptotic Distribution of the Maximum Likelihood Cointegration Rank Test Statistics', *Oxford Bulletin of Economics and Statistics*, 54, 461–71.
Park, J. and Fatemi, A.M. (1993) 'The Linkages between the Equity Markets of Pacific-Basin Countries and Those of the US, UK and Japan: A Vector Autoregression Analysis', *Global Finance Journal*, 4(1), 49–64.
Phillips, P.C. (1991) 'Optimal Inference in Cointegrated Systems', *Econometrica*, 59, 283–306.
Phillips, P.C. and Perron, P. (1988) 'Testing for a Unit Root in Time Series Regression', *Biometrika*, 57, 335–46.
Sims, C.A. (1980) 'Macroeconomics and Reality', *Econometrica*, 48, 1–48.

5

Oil Price Shocks and Emerging Stock Markets: A Generalized VAR Approach

Aktham Maghyereh

Introduction

The oil price shock of 1973 and the subsequent recession gave rise to a plethora of studies analyzing the interrelation between economic variables and oil price changes. Early studies include Pierce and Enzler (1974), Rasche and Tatom (1977), and Darby (1982), all of which documented and explained the inverse relationship between oil price increases and aggregate economic activity. Later empirical studies – such as, Hickman *et al.* (1987), Jones and Leiby (1996), Hooker (1999), Hammes and Wills (2003) and Leigh *et al.* (2003) – confirm the inverse relationship between oil prices and aggregate economic activity.

Although the bulk of the empirical research focuses on the relation between economic activity and oil price changes, it is surprising that few studies have been conducted on the relationship between financial markets and oil price shocks – and those mainly for a few industrialized countries such as the USA, UK, Japan, and Canada. For example, Jones and Kaul (1992) examine the effect of oil prices on stock prices in the USA. They find an effect of oil prices on aggregate real stock returns, including a lagged effect, in the period 1947 to 1991. In a more recent study, Jones and Kaul (1996) test whether the reaction of international stock markets to oil shocks can be justified by current and future changes in real cash flows and/or changes in expected returns. They find that in the postwar period, the reaction of US and Canadian stock prices to oil shocks can be completely accounted for by the impact of these shocks on real cash flows. In contrast, the results for both the UK and Japan are not as strong. In an important study, Huang *et al.* (1996) examine the link between daily oil future returns and daily US stock returns. The evidence suggests that oil futures returns do lead some individual oil company stock returns but oil future returns do not have much impact on general market indices. Gjerde and Saettem (1999) demonstrate that stock returns have a positive and delayed response to changes in industrial production, and that the stock market responds rationally to oil price changes in the Norwegian market. Sadorsky (1999) finds that oil prices play an important role in affecting real stock returns.

Although all of these studies recognize the importance of causal relationships between oil prices and stock market returns in some industrial countries, the results from such studies cannot be generalized to other countries. Consequently, this chapter extends the understanding of the dynamic relationship between oil prices and stock market returns by using data of 21 emerging stock markets, which helps to fill in the gap. Specifically, this chapter investigates the dynamic interactions between crude oil prices and stock prices in a large sample of emerging stock markets.

If oil plays a prominent role in an economy, one would expect changes in oil prices to be correlated with changes in stock prices. Specifically, it can be argued that if oil affects real economic activity, it will affect earnings of companies through which oil is a direct or indirect cost of operation. Thus, an increase in oil prices would cause expected earnings to decline, and this would bring about an immediate decrease in stock prices if the stock market effectively capitalizes the cash flow implications of the oil price increases. If the stock market is inefficient, stock returns might adjust slowly.

Given the evidence of stronger linkages between crude oil prices and the stock market in developed economies, this study considers this issue in the emerging economies. The study examines the dynamic linkages between crude oil prices and stock market returns in many emerging economies and, essentially, asks two questions: To what extent do price changes or returns in crude oil markets lead stock returns in emerging markets? How efficiently are innovations/shocks in the crude oil market transmitted to the stock markets in the emerging economies? In answering these questions, it is hoped that some light may be shed on the importance of the crude oil on economic output in the emerging economies. The vector autoregression (VAR) technique that is employed in this study is well suited to answering these questions. The study utilized the generalized approach to forecast error variance decomposition and impulse response analysis in favour of the more traditional orthogonalized approach. The problem with the orthogonalized approach to variance decomposition and impulse response analysis is that the order of the variables in the VAR determines the outcome of the results. The generalized approach is invariant to the ordering of the variables in the VAR and produces one unique result.

The next section describes the data used in the study and is followed by an overview of the methodological issues. The empirical evidence is presented, followed by concluding remarks.

Data

The stock market data in this chapter are obtained from Morgan Stanley Capital International (MSCI). The sample is daily and encompasses the period from 1 January 1998 to 31 April 2004, and contains US dollar denominated value-weighted stock market indices for the following 22 countries: Argentina, Brazil, Chile, China, Czech Republic, Egypt, Greece, India, Indonesia, Jordan, Korea, Malaysia, Mexico, Morocco, Hungary, Pakistan, Philippines, Poland, South Africa, Taiwan, Thailand, and Turkey. We choose to use the MSCI indices rather than other local stock price indices for several reasons. First, these indices are constructed on a consistent basis by the MSCI, making cross-country comparison more meaningful. Second, these indices are value-weighted and reflect a substantial percentage of total market capitalization which could minimize the problem of autocorrelation in returns resulting from nonsynchronous trading. Third, MSCI indices are widely employed in the literature on the basis of the degree of comparability and avoidance of dual listing.

The crude oil market is the largest commodity market in the world. Total world consumption equaled around 80 million barrels a day in 2003. Prices of three types of oil – Brent, West Texas Intermediate and Dubai – serve as a benchmark for other types of crude oil. Processing costs, and therefore prices of oil, depend on two important characteristics: sulphur content and density. Oil that has a low sulphur content ('sweet') and a low density ('light') is cheaper than oil that has a high sulphur content ('sour') and high density ('heavy'). For instance, the price of West Texas Intermediate is generally higher than Brent oil as it is sweeter and lighter than Brent oil. Of total world oil consumption of about 80 million barrels a day in 2003, Brent oil serves as a benchmark for about 50 million barrels a day, West Texas Intermediate for about 15 million barrels a day and Dubai for about 15 million barrels a day.

Even though price differences do exist, crude oil prices tend to move very closely together. Since Brent Oil serves as a benchmark in the crude oil market, daily closing prices of crude oil Brent are used as our primary proxy for the world price of crude oil.[1] The daily closing prices for crude oil for Brent for the period from 1 January, 1995 to 31 April, 2004 are obtained from the US Energy Information Administration. Finally, consistent with convention, all data used in this study has been transformed by taking the natural logarithm of the raw data.

Methodology

The unrestricted vector autoregression (VAR) approach used in this study was developed by Sims (1980). The VAR was developed to account for problems with intervention and transfer function analysis. This model provides a multivariate framework where changes in a particular variable are related to changes in its own lags and to changes in other variables. The VAR treats all variables as jointly endogeneous and imposes no a priori restrictions on the structural relationships, if any, between variables being analyzed. Because the VAR expresses the dependent variables in terms of only predetermined lagged variables, the VAR model is a reduced form model.

An argument that naturally arises in the context of a VAR is whether one should use levels or first differences in the VAR. Clearly, if the variables are I(0) processes, this is not an issue. The difficulty arises, however, when the variables need to be differenced to obtain a stationary process, as they almost invariably do when dealing with stock index data. Because of the information that is lost in differencing, Sims (1980) and Doan (1992) have argued against it. The majority view, highlighted by Granger and Newbold (1974) and Phillips (1986) is that stationary data should be used since non-stationary data can lead to spurious regression results. Further, Toda and

Yamamoto (1995) noted that conventional asymptotic theory is, in general, not applicable to hypothesis testing in levels VARs if the variables are integrated, say I(1). Thus, as the first step, the order of integration of the variables is tested. Tests for the presence of a unit root based on the work of Dickey and Fuller (1979, 1981), Phillips (1987), Perron (1988), Phillips and Perron (1988),[2] and Kwiatkowski *et al.* (1992)[3] are used to investigate the degree of integration of the variables used in the empirical analysis. If a I(1) process does exist, the second step involves estimation of the VAR model with first differences,[4] otherwise the VAR is estimated in levels. To determine the appropriate number of lag lengths of the VAR model, the Akaike Information Criterion (AIC) and Schwarz Bayesian Criterion (SBC) are employed.

Next, the generalized variance decomposition and generalized impulse response functions are employed to analyze the short-run dynamics of the variables. The purpose of the investigation is to find how each of emerging markets responds to shocks from the crude oil market. The forecast error of generalized variance decomposition analysis reveals information about the proportion of the movements in market returns due to its 'own' shocks versus shocks to the crude oil market. The dynamic responses of stock markets to innovations in the crude oil market can also be traced using generalized impulse response analysis. Plotting the generalized impulse response functions is one way to explore the response of a stock market to a shock either immediately or with various lags. Unlike the orthogonalized variance decomposition and impulse response functions obtained using the Choleskey factorization, the generalized variance decomposition and impulse response functions are unique solutions and invariant to the ordering of the variables in the VAR (Koop *et al.* 1996; and Pesaran and Shin, 1998).

Another argument that arises in the context of an unrestricted VAR is whether this model should be used where the variables in the VAR are cointegrated. There is a body of literature that supports the use of a vector error correction model (VECM), or cointegrating VAR if variables are integrated, I(1). Because the cointegrating vectors bind the long run behavior of the variables, the VECM is expected to produce results in the impulse response analysis and variance decomposition that more accurately reflect the relationship between the variables than the standard unrestricted VAR. It has been argued, however, that in the short run unrestricted VARs perform better than a cointegrating VAR (see, for example, Naka and Tufte 1997). Furthermore, Engle and Yoo (1987), Clements and Hendry (1995), and Hoffman and Rasche (1996) have shown that an unrestricted VAR is superior (in terms of forecast variance) to a restricted VECM at short horizons when the restriction is true. Naka and Tufte (1997) also studied the performance of VECMs and unrestricted VARs for impulse response analysis over the short run and found that the performance of the two methods is nearly identical. This suggests that abandoning vector autoregressions for short horizon work is premature, especially when one considers their low computational burden. Although Johansen multivariate cointegration analysis is carried out in this study and cointegrating relationships found, unrestricted VARs are used because of the short-term nature of the variance decomposition and impulse response analysis.

Empirical results

Table 5.1 presents the ADF, PP, and KPSS tests for the 21 stock markets indexes as well as crude oil price in levels and first differences. The results are consistent with what has been found in most of the previous literature using such types of data. Specifically, the three tests show that the logarithm of all series has a unit root, but the first differences are stationary. Given the importance of using stationary variables, these results necessitated the use of first differenced data to carry out the VAR analysis.

As we mentioned above, the interpretation of the VAR model can be brought to light through the generalized variance decomposition analysis and the estimation of the generalized impulse response functions. The results of variance decomposition are presented in Table 5.2. The reported numbers indicate the percentage of the forecast error in each stock market that can be attributed to innovations in the crude oil market at four different time horizons: one, five, 10 and 15 days ahead. The results of generalized variance decomposition analysis and generalized impulse response function provide the same conclusions regardless of order of decomposition since their estimation is independent of the ordering.

Generalized decomposition tends to suggest that the crude oil price shocks have no significant impact on any of the emerging stock markets under investigation. Specifically, in all cases the crude oil

Table 5.1 Unit root test statistics

	Level			First difference		
Variable	**ADF**	**PP**	**KPSS**	**ADF**	**PP**	**KPSS**
Argentina	−1.0213	−1.059350	2.868503*	−16.10779*	−36.35639*	0.301911
Brazil	−1.340802	−1.322677	1.356677*	−15.96791*	−30.50862*	0.178170
China	−1.135769	−0.995947	1.352201*	−13.48995*	−28.10903*	0.300083
Czech Rep.	−1.507845	−1.415059	3.047069*	−15.44634*	−32.46652*	0.310346
Egypt	−1.380252	−1.233500	3.533962*	−15.10693*	−30.53094*	0.386931
Greece	0.055037	−0.060300	2.364244*	−16.83602*	−33.51540*	0.221341
India	−0.975511	−0.949940	2.973629*	−14.61071*	−34.40020*	0.574628
Indonesia	−1.061733	−1.042059	1.278297*	−15.06973*	−31.53807*	0.260705
Jordan	−1.443447	−1.293387	1.777320*	−15.78797*	−31.22315*	0.341113
Korea	1.990497	1.909865	2.452268*	−16.18562*	−34.75652*	1.165394
Malaysia	−1.623583	−1.623583	0.767226*	−16.39859*	−34.56621*	0.108442
Mexico	−2.220190	−2.289600	0.116928	−14.64867*	−30.76145*	0.350469
Morocco	−2.496684	−2.531083	0.152985	−16.82238*	−31.48996*	0.066025
Hungary	−1.672223	−1.633622	2.867896*	−14.54562*	−30.67777*	0.631372
Pakistan	−0.981074	−0.937530	2.696080*	−15.23974*	−32.75377*	0.790860
Philippines	−0.414988	−0.483373	0.871556*	−14.69390*	−34.31985*	0.461944
Poland	−0.414988	−0.483373	1.672920*	−14.69390*	−34.31985*	0.281427
South Africa	−0.988925	−1.148104	3.231415*	−14.44769*	−30.10173*	0.232455
Taiwan	−2.512607	−2.417929	1.639268*	−16.09207*	−30.76302*	0.139440
Thailand	−1.700946	−1.693898	2.538950*	−15.29515*	−32.84183*	0.152295
Turkey	−1.381759	−1.426736	0.918657*	−15.13812*	−34.10471*	0.334150
Crude oil price	−0.896806	−1.682879	0.339658**	−24.99875*	−83.23893*	0.356574
Critical value 1%	−3.4384	−3.4384	0.7390	−3.4384	−3.4384	0.7390
Critical value 5%	−2.8643	−2.8643	0.4630	−2.8643	−2.8643	0.4630

Notes: * and ** indicate statistical significant at the 1% and 5% level, respectively. The Augmented Dickey–Fuller (ADF) and the Phillips–Perron (PP) tested the null hypothesis of that the relevant series contains a unit root I(1) against the alternative that it does not, while the Kwiatkowski– Phillips–Schmidt–Shin (KPSS) tested the null hypothesis that the series are I(0). The critical values for the ADF and PP are obtained from Dickey–Fuller (1981) while the KPSS critical values are obtained from Kwiatkowski *et al.* (1992).

shocks explain less than 2 per cent of the forecast errors' variances and, in 16 of the 21 emerging markets, this ratio falls to less than 1 per cent. Furthermore, the results show some interesting differences across countries in response to the oil market shocks, depending on the energy intensity of production. Specifically, the impact of oil shocks on stock markets is highest in the largest Asian and emerging

Table 5.2 Generalized decomposition of forecast error in emerging stock markets in response to shocks in the crude oil market

	5 days	10 days	15 days
Argentina	0.622064	0.634352	0.641797
Brazil	0.181891	0.237485	0.255282
China	0.076167	0.053178	0.045921
Czech Rep.	0.169356	0.245609	0.270753
Egypt	0.065641	0.086715	0.093538
Greece	1.146167	1.393299	1.546380
India	0.212965	0.731871	1.074984
Indonesia	0.014805	0.036561	0.049455
Jordan	0.172647	0.586863	0.855067
Korea	1.703050	2.020706	2.028246
Malaysia	1.375227	2.005126	2.384872
Mexico	0.042720	0.178622	0.261737
Morocco	0.022182	0.015533	0.012700
Hungary	0.117332	0.076421	0.059594
Pakistan	0.110283	0.272700	0.370517
Philippines	0.041558	0.036562	0.034073
Poland	0.041558	0.036562	0.034073
South Africa	1.130735	1.734103	2.051688
Taiwan	1.115818	1.353554	1.501680
Thailand	0.157792	0.530656	0.817114
Turkey	2.101294	2.381148	2.568307

Europe economies, as they have higher energy intensity production than most other emerging economies. For example, at the 15-day horizons, the percentage of error variance of a stock market explained by innovations in the crude oil market is 2.57 for Turkey, followed by 2.38 for Malaysia. The Polish market appears to be the least influenced by the oil market.

Turning to the question of how effectively innovations may transmit from the oil market to the emerging stock markets, Figure 5.1 plots the responses of each of the 21 emerging stock markets to a one standard error shock in the oil market. The plots in Figure 5.1 show that innovations in the oil market are slowly transmitted in all of the emerging stock markets with markets responding to the oil shock two days after it has occurred. The speed with which the responses taper off to zero after the initial shock is felt by most markets on day 4. Only six markets (Argentina, Brazil, China, Czech Republic, Egypt and

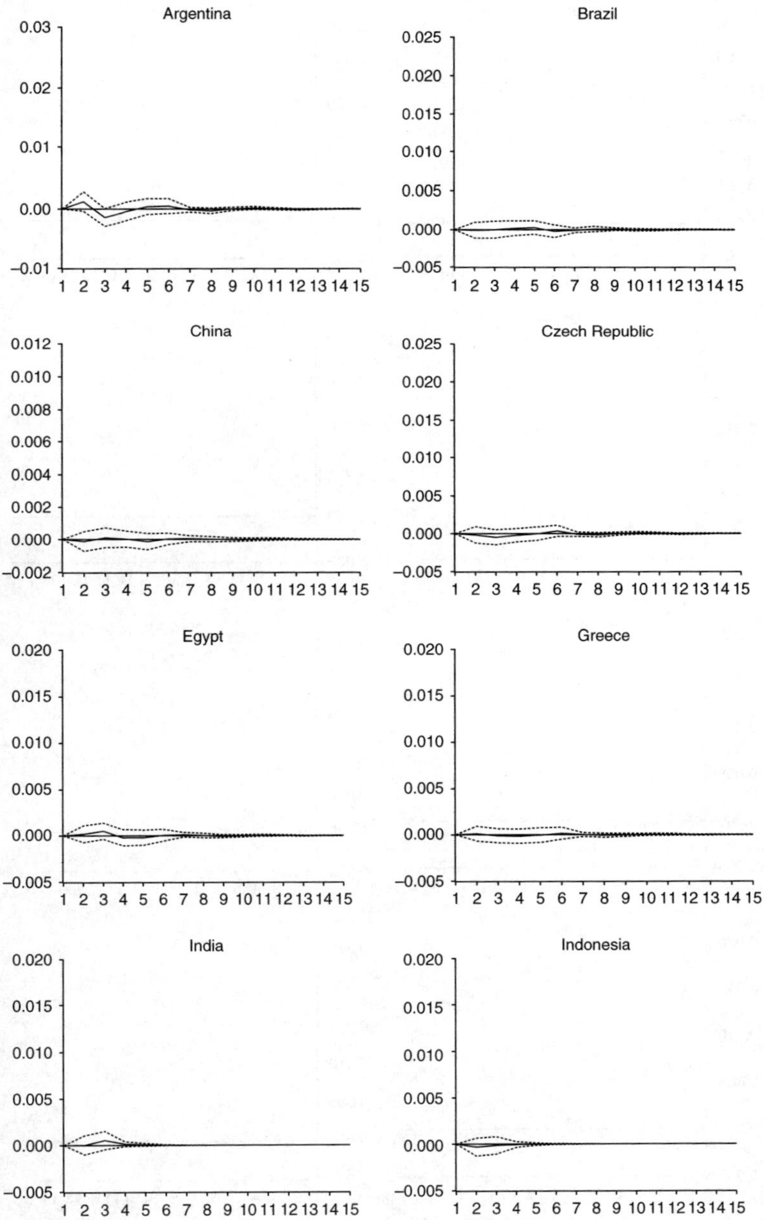

Figure 5.1 Time paths generalized impulse response to a one standard error shock in the crude oil market

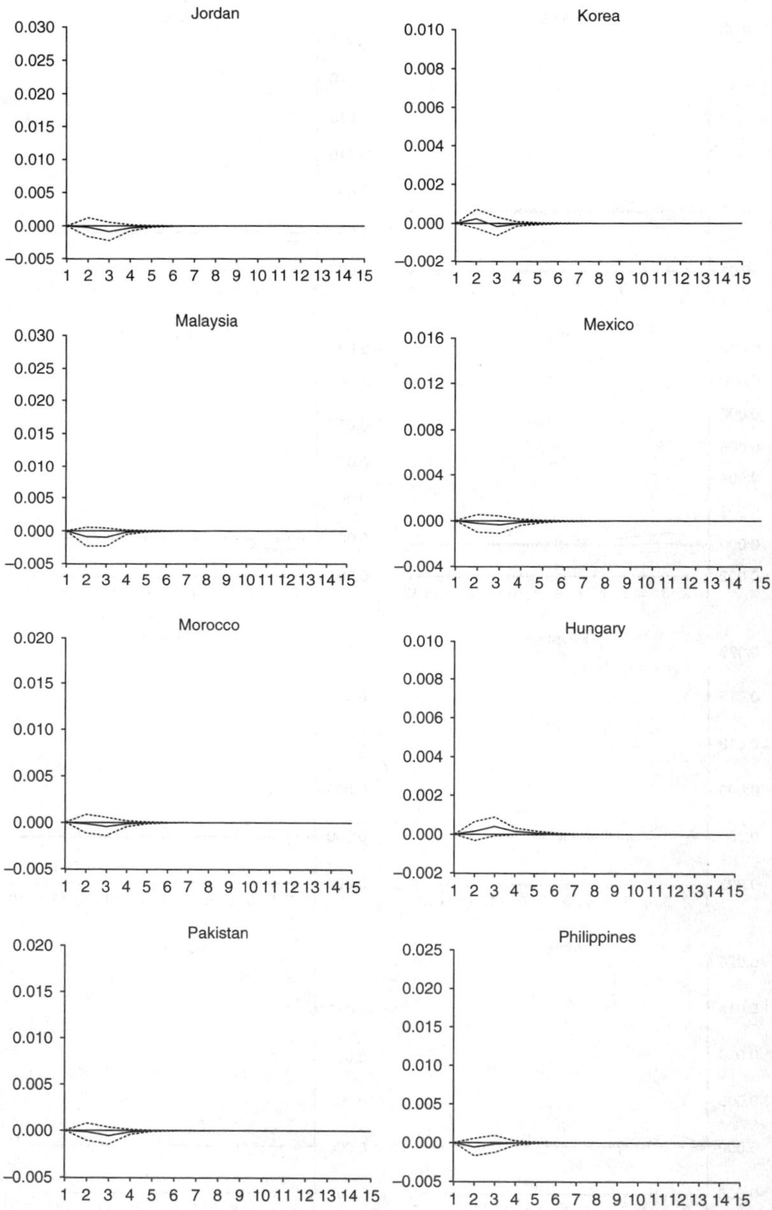

Figure 5.1 Continued

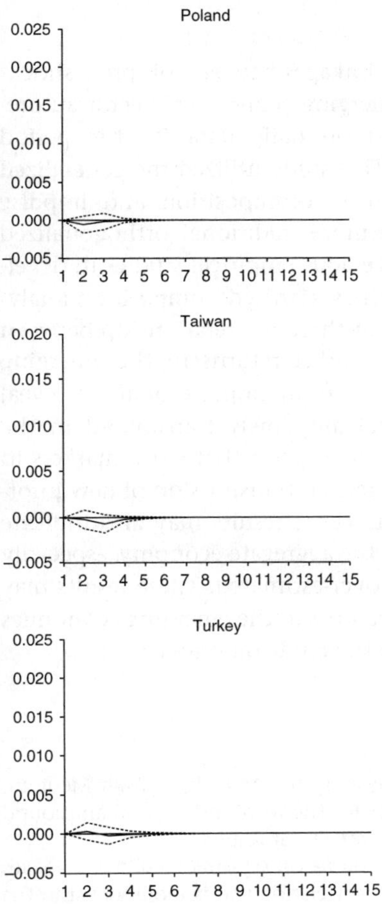

Figure 5.1 Continued

Greece) showed continued responses until day 7. These results may indicate that the emerging markets are inefficient in transmitting innovations/shocks in the oil market. The inefficiency in responses to a shock in the oil market is also reflected in the inaccuracy of the initial response to the shock. However, the small size of the responses (between 0.00051 to 0.00126 on day 2) reflects that the oil market is very weak in influencing stock markets in emerging economies.

Conclusion

This study examines the dynamic linkages between oil price shocks and stock market returns in 21 emerging economies. Vector autoregression (VAR) analysis is carried on daily data for the period 1 January 1998 to 31 April 2004. This study utilized the generalized approach to forecast error variance decomposition and impulse response analysis in favor of the more traditional orthogonalized approach. Inconsistent with the previous empirical studies in developed economies, the results from the variance decomposition analysis provided very weak evidence that there is a relationship between crude oil price shocks and stock market returns in the emerging economies. Furthermore, the results from impulse analysis reveal that innovations in the oil market are slowly transmitted in the emerging stock markets. These results suggest that stock markets in the emerging economies are inefficient in transmission of new information concerning the oil market. These results may also indicate that the importance of oil price for the aggregate economy, especially in emerging economies, is greatly over-estimated. These results may also suggest that the stock market returns in the emerging economies do not rationally signal changes in the crude oil prices.

Notes

1. We also estimated the results using daily for Arab light, Arab Medium, Dubai and West Texas as alternatives for the world price of oil and found these measures did not substantively affect our results.
2. This version of the test is an extension of the Dickey-Fuller test, which makes a semi-parametric correlation for autocorrelation and is more robust in the case of weakly autocorrelated and heteroskedastic regression residuals.
3. The KPSS procedure assumes the univariate series can be decomposed into the sum of a deterministic trend, random walk, and stationary I(0) disturbance and is based on a Lagrange Multiplier score testing principle. This test reverses the null and alternative hypothesis. A finding favourable to a unit root in this case requires strong evidence against the hypothesis of stationarity.
4. Earlier studies of stock returns have shown that stock returns exhibit a number of important seasonalities (e.g. January and weekend effects). These sesonalities are accounted for in our analysis by introducing dummy variables in the VAR model. Furthermore, important events in oil and equity markets during the period under investigation are the September 11 attacks and its subsequent and the US invitation of Iraq on March 19.

Oil and equity markets fluctuated dramatically as a consequence of these events, therefore these events are also accounted for in the analysis by introducing dummy variables.

References

Clements, M.P. and Hendry, D.F. (1995) 'Forecasting in Cointegrated Systems', *Journal of Applied Econometrics*, 10, 127–46.

Darby, M.R. (1982) 'The Price of Oil and World Inflation and Recession', *American Economic Review*, 72, 738–51.

Dickey, D. and Fuller, W.A. (1979) 'Distribution of the Estimates for Autoregressive Time Series with a Unit Root', *Journal of the American Statistical Association*, 74, 427–31.

Dickey, D. and Fuller, W.A. (1981) 'Likelihood Ratio Statistics for Autoregressive Time Series with a Unit Root', *Econometrica*, 49, 1057–72.

Doan, T. (1992) *RATS User's Manual* (Evanston, IL: Estima).

Engle, R.F. and Yoo, B.S. (1987) 'Forecasting and Testing in Cointegrated Systems', *Journal of Econometrics*, 35, 143–59.

Gjerde, O. and Sættem, F. (1999) 'Causal Relations among Stock Returns and Macroeconomic Variables in a Small, Open Economy', *Journal of International Financial Markets, Institutions and Money*, 9(1), 61–74.

Granger, C.W.J and Newbold, P. (1974) 'Spurious Regressions in Econometrics', *Journal of Econometrics*, 2, 111–20.

Hammes, D. and Wills, D. (2003) 'Black Gold: The End of Bretton Woods and the Oil Price Shocks of the 1970s', Working paper, University of Hawaii Hilo.

Hickman, B., Huntington, H. and Sweeney, J. (1987) *Macroeconomic Impacts of Energy Shocks* (Amsterdam: North-Holland).

Hoffman, D.L. and Rasche, R.H. (1996) 'Assessing Forecast Performance in a Cointegrated System', *Journal of Applied Econometrics*, 11, 495–517.

Hooker, M. (1999) 'Are Oil Shocks Inflationary? Asymmetric and Nonlinear Specifications versus Changes in Regime', Working paper, Federal Reserve Board of Governors.

Huang, R.D., Masulis, R.W. and Stoll, H.R. (1996) 'Energy Shocks and Financial Markets', 27, *Journal of Future Markets*, 16, 1–25.

Jones, C.M. and Kaul, G. (1992) 'Oil and Stock Markets', *Journal of Finance*, 51, 463–91.

Jones, C.M. and Kaul, G. (1996) 'Oil and Stock Markets', *Journal of Finance*, 51, 463–91.

Jones, D.W. and Leiby, P. (1996) 'The Macroeconomic Impacts of Oil Price Shocks: A Review of the Literature and Issues', Working paper, Oak Ridge National Laboratory.

Koop, G., Pesaran, M. and Potter, S. (1996) 'Impulse Response Analysis in Nonlinear Multivariate Models', *Journal of Econometrics*, 74, 119–47.

Kwiatkowski, D., Phillips, P.C.B., Schmidt, P. and Shim, Y. (1992) 'Testing the Null Hypothesis of Stationarity Against the Alternative of a Unit Root', *Journal of Econometrics*, 54, 159–78.

Leigh, A., Wolfers, J. and Zitzewitz, E. (2003) 'What do Financial Markets Think about the War of Iraq?', Working paper, Stanford Graduate School of Business.

Naka, A. and Tufte, D. (1997) 'Examining Impulse Response Functions in Cointegrated Systems', *Applied Economics*, 29, 1593–603.

Perron, P. (1988) 'Trends and Random Walks in Macroeconomic Time: Series Further Evidence from a New Approach', *Journal of Economic Dynamics and Control*, 12, 297–332.

Pesaran, H.H. and Shin, Y. (1998) 'Generalized Impulse Response Analysis in Linear Multivariate models', *Economics Letters*, 58(1), 17–29.

Phillips, P.C.B. (1986) 'Understanding Spurious Regressions in Econometrics', *Journal of Econometrics*, 33, 311–40.

Phillips, P.C.B. (1987) 'Time Series Regression with a Unit Root', *Econometrica*, 55, 277–347.

Phillips, P.C.B. and Perron, P. (1988) 'Testing for a Unit Root in Time Series Regression', *Biometrika*, 75, 335–46.

Pierce, J.L. and Enzler, J.J. (1974) 'The Effects of External Inflationary Shocks', *Brookings Papers on Economic Activity*, 1, 13–61.

Pierce, J.L. and Jared, J.E. (1974) 'The Effects of External Inflationary Shocks', *Brooking Papers on Economic Activity*, 1, 13–61.

Rasche, R.H. and Tatom, J.A. (1977) 'The Effect of the New Energy Regime on Economic Capacity, Production and Prices', *Economic Review*, 59, 2–12.

Sadorsky, P. (1999) 'Oil Price Shocks and Stock Market Activity', *Energy Economics*, 21, 449–69.

Sims, C.A. (1980) 'Macroeconomics and Reality', *Econometrica*, 48, 1–48.

Toda, B.H. and Yamamoto, T. (1995) 'Statistical Inference in Vector Autoregressions with Possibly Integrated Process', *Journal of Econometrics*, 66, 225–50.

6

Reactions to Regulatory Changes and Policy Adjustments in an Emerging Stock Market: China

Jing Kong and Ding Lu

Introduction

When government changes rules and policies regarding stock market regulation, share prices are likely to respond with significant and unusual movements. China's stock market is no exception to such reactions. In this chapter, we investigate those market reactions in China's stock exchange during the period of 1995–2003.

Stock market response to the arrival of marketwide public information has been verified by a considerable volume empirical evidence. For instance, Chan and Wei (1996) found that political news increased stock volatility for all types of shares in Hong Kong, but a consistent pattern of impact of favourable or unfavourable news on returns could be observed only for shares other than the so-called 'red-chip' shares of Chinese-based companies. Kim and Mei (2001) also used Hong Kong stock data to calculate the frequent association between the largest market movements of returns and major political news. Their empirical results reveal an asymmetric pattern of impact on return volatility between good news and bad news. Edmonds and Kutan (2002) used disaggregated dummies combined with GARCH (1, 1) to identify the significant impact of macroeconomic announcements on Japanese stock returns during the period 1990–99. Kutan and Yuan (2003) found that, among three categories of public macroeconomic announcements, trade-related announcements have the most significant impact on stock returns in China's stock markets.

To study market response to regulatory changes, a number of studies, including Umlauf (1993) and Jones and Seguin (1997), have investigated the impact of announced changes in the rate of stamp duty or transaction commissions on stock price movements.

China provides an ideal case for investigating the effects of government regulatory changes and policy adjustments on stock market behaviour. Since its launch around 1990, this emerging market has been exposed to frequent announcements of policy and regulatory changes as the whole economy has been dramatically transformed from a centrally planned system to a market-based one. Given the intensity and frequency of these information shocks, the substantial daily movements of China's stock prices provide a database with the potential to generate robust observations of market reaction patterns. What makes the issue more fascinating is the segmentation of China's stock market, where two classes of shares, the A-shares and the B-shares, are traded. The A-shares, denominated and payable in Chinese currency, can be held and traded only by domestic investors. The B-shares, quoted and payable in US or Hong Kong dollars, had not been openly accessible to indigenous investors until early 2001.

The existing literature has explored the impact of only one or several regulatory events in this emerging market. Ma (1996) showed that the reactions to the regulatory market support policies announced on 30 June 1993 were much stronger in the A-share market than in the B-share market. Su and Fleisher (1998) reported that the removal of a 5 per cent price ceiling on 22 May 1992 was followed by increased return volatility in the Shanghai A-share index. Karolyi and Li (2003) studied price responses to the regulatory change of opening the B-share market to domestic investors on 19 February 2001.

In this study, we group the regulatory changes and policy adjustments during the sample period, from 1995 to 2003, into six major categories. To examine whether regulatory changes and policy adjustments are important in causing major surprises in stock markets, we first detect dates with return outliers and then identify the various events that cause these return spikes. In this way, we can further investigate the percentage of outliers that are caused by the regulatory changes and compare the return variances in the sub-markets before and after the adjustments of regulatory event related return outliers. A modified GARCH-M model combined with dummy variables is used to investigate: (1) whether market reactions around the event day are of any significant patterns; (2) whether the market responses are different in the A-share and B-share sub-markets;[1] (3) whether the market responses are different to different types of regulation events.

The next section is an overview of China's stock market institutions. We go on to describe the data sources and present a summary of descriptive statistics. The subsequent section discusses the outlier detection procedure and relates return outliers with the events of major regulatory changes and policy adjustments. We then present a modified GARCH-M model and its estimated results that testify to the impacts of various categories of events on market movements. The chapter closes with a summary and discusses the main findings.

Overview of China's stock market

There are two official national stock exchanges in the People's Republic of China – the Shanghai Stock Exchange (SHSE), founded on 19 December 1990, and Shenzhen Stock Exchange (SZSE), inaugurated on 3 July 1991. Trading is continuously conducted by an order-drive computerized matching system. On SHSE, orders are automatically matched on a time–price priority basis, while on the SZSE, orders are matched on a price–time–order priority basis. Apart from providing locations and facilities for trading, the main duties of the exchanges also include formulating trading rules; publishing trading information; reporting to regulatory and supervisory authorities; and taking temporary measures to suspend or stop trading. By the end of 2003, there were 1287 companies listed on China's mainland exchanges.

According to China's corporate law, there are several types of shares that companies can issue. The term 'state shares' refers to shares held by government agencies or authorized institutions on behalf of the state. 'Legal person shares' refers to shares of a joint stock company owned by another company or institution with appropriate legal status. 'Individual shares', or A-shares, refers to shares that are restricted to Chinese citizens for trading and transfers. The term 'foreign capital shares' includes the B-shares and overseas listed shares (the 'H-shares' traded in Hong Kong, the 'N-shares' traded in New York and the 'S-shares' traded in Singapore, and so on).

Among these types of shares, only A- and B-shares can be traded in the domestic SHSE and SZSE. However, they were intentionally segmented from the very inception of China's stock market. A-shares are restricted to domestic investors and traded in China's currency, Renminbi, while B-shares are restricted to foreign investors and traded in U.S. dollar at SHSE and in Hong Kong dollar at SZSE.[2] A- and B-shares have exactly the same ownership and dividend rights. Apart from the ownership restriction and trading currency difference, there are a number of differences between A- and B-shares (Gao and Tse, 2001). First, the number of listed stocks, issued shares, the market capitalization, and the trading volume of the A-shares is much greater than for B-shares. Second, for the A-shares, settlement takes place on the same day (T+0) of a transaction between members of exchanges, and the next day (T+1) between the broker and his customer. As for B-shares, the settlement takes place three days after the day of a transaction (T+3). Third, the A-share market is overwhelmed by individual investors, while the B-share market has much larger participation by institutional investors. Fourth, the information release requirements for companies with B-shares are higher than those for companies issuing A-shares only. The financial statements of companies issuing B-shares must follow International Accounting Standards (IASs) and are audited by internationally recognized audit firms, while those of companies issuing A-shares are audited by domestic CPA firms, which are still in the development stage, in accordance with the General Accepted Accounting Principles (GAAP). As for marketwide information, Xu (2000) pointed out that foreign investors seem to have better access to timely updates on the Chinese economy through media such as Reuters, Bloomberg News, and other financial information services. Finally, according to data in the China Securities and Futures Statistical Yearbook 2003, the average P/E ratio for the A-shares is much higher than that of the B-shares.

The institution building process of China's stock market has been heavily influenced by the political–economic dynamism in the country's market oriented transition. The establishing of the State Council Securities Committee (SCSC) and the Chinese Securities Regulatory Commission (CSRC) in October 1992 was a milestone in this process. From October 1992 to mid-1998, the SCSC was the immediate supervisory body over the CSRC, which was set up as a specialized independent regulatory body in charge of the day-to-day monitoring of the securities market and market participants. When the SCSC was dissolved in 1998, the CSRC was upgraded to the equivalent rank of a ministry, with extensive authorities, including a supervisory role over brokerage houses and stock exchanges in Shanghai and Shenzhen. China's first Securities Law, which took effect in July 1999, further strengthened the CSRC's supervisory power. However, as observed by Walter and Howie (2001), there had been a continuous power struggle among the People's Bank of China (PBOC), the Ministry of Finance (MOF) and other bureaucracies over the control of the securities industry. So, despite the organizational restructure, the regulatory framework still remains fragmented. What makes things worse, is the conflicting policy missions assigned to the CSRC. As noted by Heilmann (2002), the agency's policy mission to provide preferential capital access for state-owned enterprises and to increase the value of state assets constantly conflicts its role of being an impartial supervisory and regulatory authority.

Against the backdrop of this evolving regulatory framework, China's stock market has been seen as a 'policy-driven market'. Initially, the stock market was developed for the reform of state-owned enterprises (SOEs). The government selected certain SOEs to be corporatized and listed in the stock market. The segmentation of the tradable and non-tradable shares ensures the continuous control by the state. The segmentation of A- and B-shares reflects the official policy of restricting the control of domestic companies by foreign investors and prevention of manipulation of China's emerging market by foreign players. Since its launch, China's stock market has manifested a particular regulatory style distinctively different from that of other stock markets (Heilmann 2002). The regulatory policies are imbued with the spirit of state planning, state control and state interest. Frequent regulatory changes have been oriented towards supporting the SOEs. Direct state interventions in trading have been a norm, featuring imposition of daily price change limits, the raising of ownership transfer stamp duties, and various administrative measures in the name of market-boosting policies and disciplinary supervision. Sometimes the authorities even attempt to talk up the market with the help of state-controlled media. There have been periods of intensified regulatory changes and policy adjustments. In 1999, for instance, the authorities, in a bid to revitalize the gloomy market, opened more financial facilities for brokerage firms and lifted a ban on SOEs, listed companies and issuance companies from trading in the securities markets.

Data source and descriptive statistics

The daily closing prices of four indices (i.e. Shanghai Stock Exchange (SE) A-share index (SHA), Shenzhen SE A-share index (SZA), Shanghai SE B-share index (SHB), and Shenzhen SE B-share index (SZB)) are used as proxies for market movements. All the index price data are obtained from Datasteam. Events of regulatory changes and interest-rate adjustments are results of research of the *People's Daily* (http://www.peopledaily.com.cn/), *China Securities* (an official publication by the China Securities Regulation Commission), and *China Securities Bulletin* (a Hong Kong-based press publication available from Factive information service provided by Reuters and Dow Jones).[3] Should a chain of similar regulatory events occur on consecutive days, the first day would be chosen as the event day if these events can be identified as relating to the same issue. The data cover the period 2 January 1995 to 31 December 2003.[4]

Table 6.1 gives a summary of the descriptive statistics of the daily returns for SHA, SHB, SZA and SZB indices, which are calculated as the log difference change in the price index:

$$R_t = (\ln P_{it} - \ln P_{t-1}) \times 100 \tag{6.1}$$

where R_t is the daily return for the market index and P_t is the closing price index on day t.

The results indicate that the mean returns for all the four submarkets are quite small, and not significantly different from zero. The standard deviations of Shanghai and Shenzhen A-share markets are lower than those of Shanghai and Shenzhen B-share markets, showing that B-shares are more volatile than A-shares during the sample period. The parameters for skewness are all significantly positive, indicating that stock market returns are not symmetrically distributed. The coefficients of Kurtosis are also very high, suggesting that extreme daily return movements are frequently observed in all SHA, SZA, SHB and SZB markets. The Jarque–Bera statistics that test the hypothesis of normal distribution are rejected at a very high level. Table 6.2 provides a correlation matrix of market returns.

Table 6.1 Descriptive statistics of market returns, 1995–2003

	SHA	SZA	SHB	SZB
Mean	0.036	0.043	0.022	0.049
Median	0.000	0.000	0.000	0.000
Maximum	27.851	25.942	12.184	12.448
Minimum	−18.427	−19.632	−13.085	−16.699
Standard deviation	1.895	1.984	2.255	2.398
Skewness	0.996	0.387	0.432	0.246
Kurtosis	31.020	23.695	8.234	9.553
Jarque–Bera	77167	41943	2752	4223
p-value for JB	(0.0000)	(0.0000)	(0.0000)	(0.0000)

Source: Datastream

Table 6.2 Correlation matrix of market returns, 1995–2003

	R_SHA	R_SZA	R_SHB	R_SZB
R_SHA	1.0000			
R_SZA	0.8902	1.0000		
R_SHB	0.4110	0.4026	1.0000	
R_SZB	0.4361	0.4372	0.7582	1.0000

Source: Datastream

All coefficients are highly significant. At the same time, the correlations between the two A- (B-)share market indices are almost twice of those between A- and B-share indices on the same exchanges.

The regulatory events are divided into six categories: (1) market-boosting policy (except for transaction cost cuts) (e.g. the CSRC granted the permission to SOEs and listed companies to enter the secondary securities market on 9 September 1999); (2) disciplinary action and strengthening of supervision (e.g. the People's Bank of China (PBOC) announced the prohibition of bank funds to be used for stock trading on 6 June 1997); (3) supportive talks by officials and commentary in press (e.g. the top securities regulator – Zhou Xiaochuan talked up the market on 5 August 1998); (4) market expansion (for only A- or B-share) (e.g. the CSRC announced a new annual quota of RMB 5.5 billion of A-share listing on 15 June 1995 and unveiled a new list of 18 candidates who might issue B-shares on

9 February 1998); (5) transaction cost adjustment (stamp duty, commission, etc.) (e.g. the Ministry of Finance (MOF) announced the stamp duty for A- and B-shares reduced to 0.2 per cent on 16 November 2001); (6) market expansion (for both A- and B-shares) (e.g. China unveiled rules aimed at cutting the state's holdings in firms to raise funds for social security on 14 June 2001). Because some regulation changes are only for the A-share market, some are only for the B-share market, while some others are for both markets, the event samples for the A- and B-share are different for categories (1)–(5). During the sample period, the PBOC cut the interest rate nine times and State Administration of Taxation (SAT) announced the imposition of a 20 per cent tax on bank interest on 26 July 1999. These announcements are also included in the empirical investigate as control variables for their possible impact on market movements.[5]

Detecting outliers in market returns

Outlier detection procedure is widely used in literature to identify the external influences on time series. Lo and Chan (2000), for instance, used a modified outlier identification methodology to analyze the large shocks in stock markets in the Greater China area – Hong Kong, Shanghai B-shares, Shenzhen B-shares and Taiwan. They observed more outliers in China's B-share markets than in the other markets, and found that most outliers in China's stock market seem to be driven by local events. To assess to what degree there is a coincidence between return outliers and regulatory changes or policy adjustments, in this section we first detect market shocks and then identify the events that caused the market hikes. The methodology used to identify large market movements is a modified ARIMA outlier detection procedure following that of Vandaele (1983), which can be used to identify the level shifts, temporal pulses and time trend in a given time series.[6]

Results of the procedure indicate no level shift and time trend in market returns and all outlier returns appear to be temporal.[7] We define a match if the event day falls on the same day as or the day before the date of the return spike. Table 6.3 shows the classification of the causes of the largest fifty return outliers in the four sub-markets.[8] It can be seen that a large percentage of market hikes were consequences of authorities' regulatory changes and policy adjustments – which caused about 70 per cent of return outliers for the SHA, SZA and SZB markets

Table 6.3 Classification of 'causes' of return outliers, 1995–2003

	SHA	SZA	SHB	SZB
Regulatory change and policy adjustment	**36 (72%)**	**33 (66%)**	**26 (52%)**	**34 (68%)**
Market-boosting policy (except for transaction cost cut)	8 (16%)	8 (16%)	9 (18%)	10 (20%)
Disciplinary action and strengthening of supervision	13 (26%)	9 (18%)	5 (10%)	7 (14%)
Supportive talk by officials and commentary in press	5 (10%)	6 (12%)	3 (6%)	11 (22%)
Market expansion (for only A- or B-shares)	6 (12%)	4 (8%)	2 (4%)	1 (12%)
Transaction cost adjustment	3 (12%)	3 (12%)	2 (12%)	0 (0%)
Market expansion (for both A- and B-shares)	7 (14%)	8 (16%)	6 (12%)	6 (12%)
Political events	**3 (6%)**	**4 (8%)**	**5 (10%)**	**4 (8%)**
Domestic (Mainland) China	1 (2%)	1 (2%)	0 (0%)	0 (0%)
Hong Kong and Taiwan Region	2 (4%)	3 (6%)	4 (8%)	3 (6%)
International	0 (0%)	0 (0%)	1 (2%)	1 (2%)
Market rumours/expectation	**5 (10%)**	**5 (10%)**	**9 (18%)**	**7 (14%)**
Government regulation change and policy adjustment	4 (8%)	3 (6%)	8 (16%)	6 (12%)
Political issue	1 (2%)	2 (4%)	1 (2%)	1 (2%)
Macroeconomic data announcement	**1 (2%)**	**0 (0%)**	**2 (4%)**	**1 (2%)**
Chinese New Year holiday	**2 (4%)**	**2 (4%)**	**2 (4%)**	**2 (4%)**
Fluctuation in other markets	**0 (0%)**	**1 (2%)**	**6 (12%)**	**2 (4%)**
Others	**2 (4%)**	**2 (4%)**	**3 (6%)**	**1 (2%)**
No specific reason	**2 (4%)**	**5 (10%)**	**1 (2%)**	**2 (4%)**

Note: The percentages for all 'causes' categories add up to more than 100% since certain dates are coded under multiple 'causes'.

and above 50 per cent for the SHB market. Under this category of causes, the market-boosting policy (except for transaction cost cuts) and disciplinary action and strengthening of supervision seem to have more impacts on markets. It is interesting to see that the events of supportive talks by officials and commentary in the press also have significant impacts on markets. Several of the largest market shifts were generated by rumours/expectation about regulatory changes and policy adjustments. As expected, domestic political events in mainland China had greater influence on the A-share market. In contrast, international/Hong Kong and Taiwan political events had greater impact on the B-share markets.[9] So had fluctuations in other markets, in most cases, in the Hong Kong market. Macroeconomic data announcements seem to have shocked the markets in only a few cases.[10] Another interesting finding here is that for each market, two return outliers occurred during the first trading days after the long Chinese-New-Year public holidays. In sum, we find that the sudden shifts in China's stock market returns were closely associated with regulatory changes or policy adjustment announcements. The B-share markets, especially SHB, appear to be considerably more sensitive to movements in international markets than the A-share markets.

We compute the sample variance of SHA, SZA, SHB and SZB before and after the adjustments of return outliers. The comparison is showed in Table 6.4. The B-share markets are more volatile than the

Table 6.4 Sample variance for index returns, 1995–2003

	SHA	SZA	SHB	SZB
Without outlier adjustment [a]	3.5892	3.9349	5.0865	5.7504
Adjusted for the largest 50 outliers [b]	1.9725	2.2469	3.4156	3.8516
Percentage of variance reduction by excluding the largest 50 outliers [(b–a)/a]	−.4504	−.4290	−.3285	−.3302
Adjusted for outliers related to regulatory changes [c]	2.2792	2.6206	4.1598	4.4125
% of variance reduction by excluding the regulatory-change related outliers [(c–a)/a]	−.3650	−.3340	−.1822	−.2327
% of the largest-50-outlier related variance reduction that is associated with regulatory changes ((c–a)/(b–a))	.8104	.7786	.5546	.7047

A-share markets – a phenomenon also indicated by the standard deviation values reported in Table 6.1. As shown in Table 6.4, the largest 50 outliers account for about 30–45 per cent of the sample variance. Of the variance reduction associated with the largest 50 outliers, 81 per cent, 78 per cent, 55 per cent and 70 per cent can be attributed to regulatory change related return outliers in SHA, SZA, SHA and SHB respectively. These results suggest that China's stock markets are susceptible to large shocks, most of which can be attributed to government regulatory changes and policy adjustments.

The timing and size of the outliers are plotted as time lines in Figure 6.1. For each market, the number of positive shocks and number of negative shocks are almost the same in the sample period. The time lines clearly show similar patterns in the SHA and SZA markets, and different patterns between A- and B-share sub-markets on the Shanghai or Shenzhen Stock Exchanges. These patterns suggest that the A- and B-share sub-markets are exposed to different marketwide information shocks. Such an asymmetric exposure may be the reason behind the continuous segmentation between the A- and B-share sub-markets observed by a number of studies in the literature.

Modified GARCH-M model

We now test the market reactions to various kinds of regulatory changes and policy adjustments in a more systematic way. First, we estimate abnormal returns and return volatility at the same time by using a modified generalized autoregressive conditional heteroscedasticity in mean (GARCH-M) model (e.g. Nelson 1991). Under the traditional GARCH (1,1)-M methodology, two distinct specifications for mean and variance are made:

$$R_t = \alpha_0 + \alpha_1\sigma + \varepsilon_t \tag{6.2}$$

where $\varepsilon_t = \sigma_t z_t$, and

$$\sigma^2 = \beta_0 + \beta_1\sigma_{t-1}^2 + \beta_2\varepsilon_{t-1}^2 \tag{6.3}$$

where $\beta_0, \beta_1, \beta_2 > 0$ and $\beta_1 + \beta_2 < 1$

We modify the above GARCH-M model by adding AR(1) or MA(1) item in the conditional mean equation when needed.[11] Since empirical

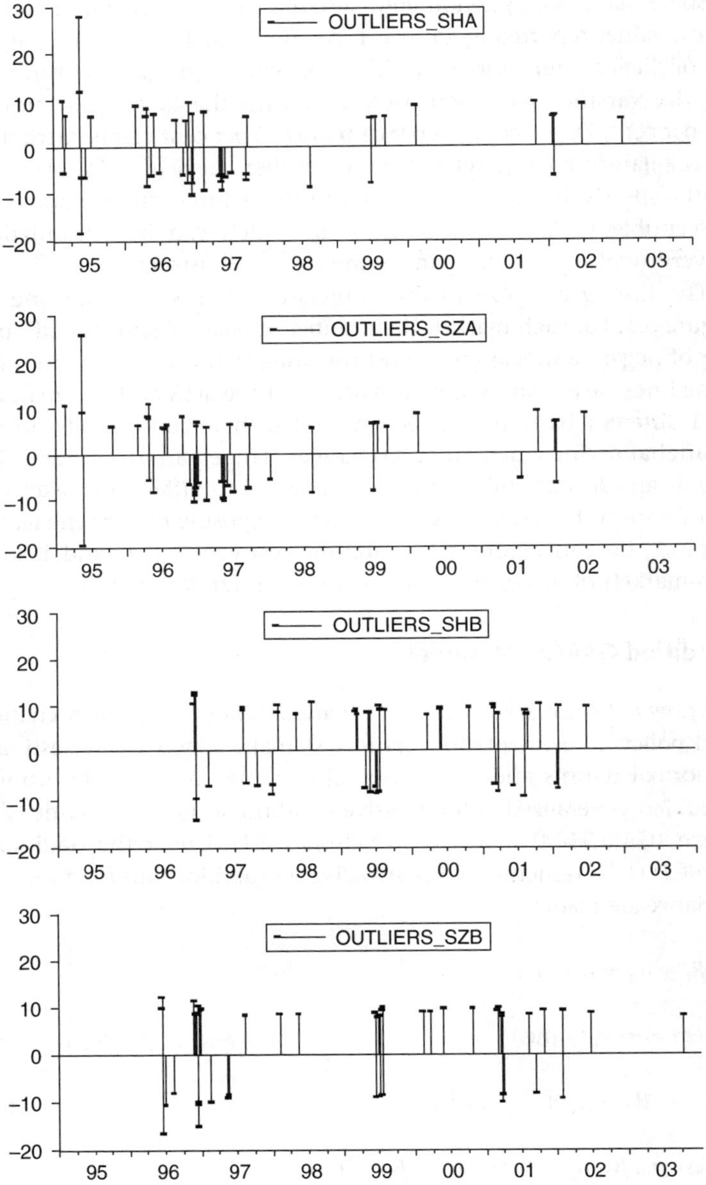

Figure 6.1 Size and timings of the detected return outliers

Table 6.5 Estimation results of the GARCH (1, 1)-M model (without dummies)

Coefficient	SHA	SZA	SHB	SZB
Mean equation				
GARCH	0.0151	0.0230*	0.0232*	0.0190*
Constant	−0.0114	−0.0341	−0.1228	−0.0596
AR(1)/MA(1)	NA	NA	0.1093***	0.1162***
Variance equation				
Constant	0.1133***	0.1802***	0.1033***	0.1765***
ARCH(1)	0.1556***	0.2512***	0.2023***	0.2933***
GARCH(1)	0.7855***	0.6789***	0.7702***	0.6619***

Note: *** and * indicates t-value significant at 1 per cent and 10 per cent level respectively.

evidence shows that daily stock returns are not normally distributed, here we assume that z_t follows t-distribution. Table 6.5 reports the estimation results of the GARCH-M models without dummy variables. Three out of four coefficients for the GARCH in mean term turn out to be significant and positive, giving evidence of the positive relationship between the return and volatility. The sums of the ARCH and GARCH coefficients in the variance equation are all very close to unity, which indicate that a volatility shock persistently raises the stock market volatility.

The abnormal returns (the residuals) and the conditional standard deviations for the SHA, SZA, SHB and SZB markets from 1995 to 2003 are plotted in Figure 6.2. Dashed lines mark the days on which the return outliers match the marketwide information of regulatory changes and policy adjustments. It can be seen that all the four submarkets are marked by frequent volatile spikes, of which most occurred on events of regulatory changes and policy adjustments. They all have volatile returns clustered on the days associated with some regulatory changes – such as the imposition of a 10 per cent trading price range limit in December 1996, and the series of policy announcements for the scheme to reduce State held shares from the end of 2001 to the first half of 2002. In some other cases, however, the regulatory events were relevant for just one category of the submarkets – such as lifting the ban on domestic investors to trade in B-shares in February 2001. It is also worth noting that B-share markets appear to be more volatile than the A-share markets, a phenomenon

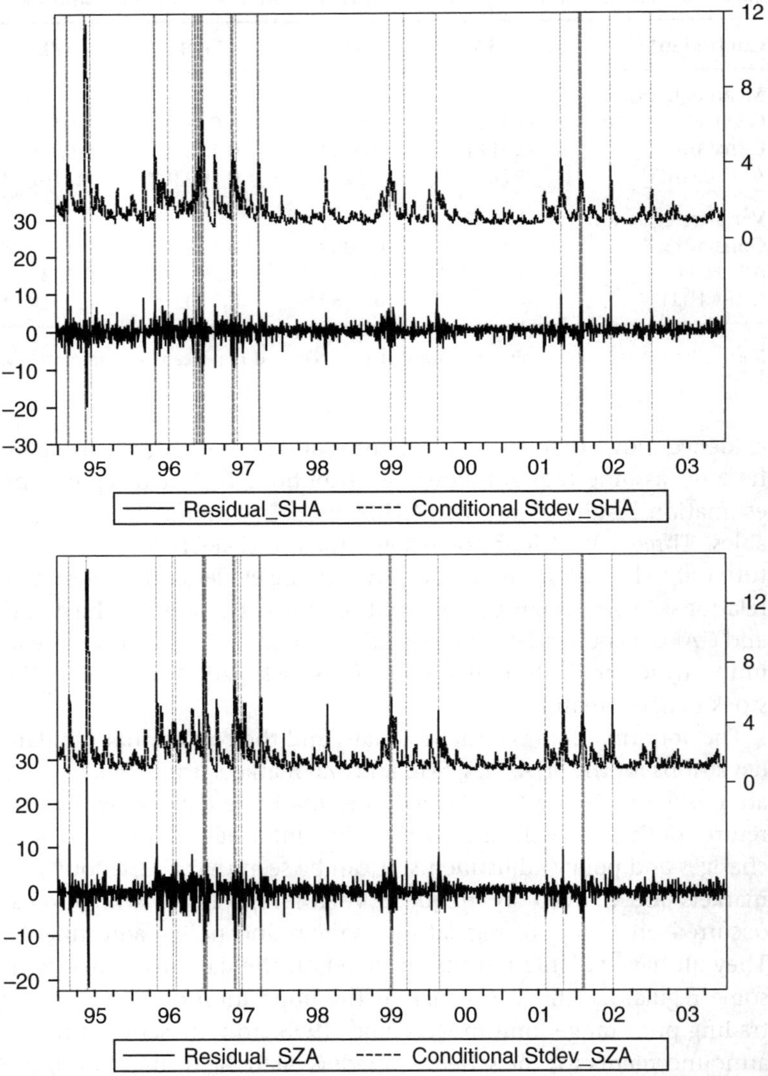

Figure 6.2 Regulatory event days and GARCH model residual and conditional standard deviation

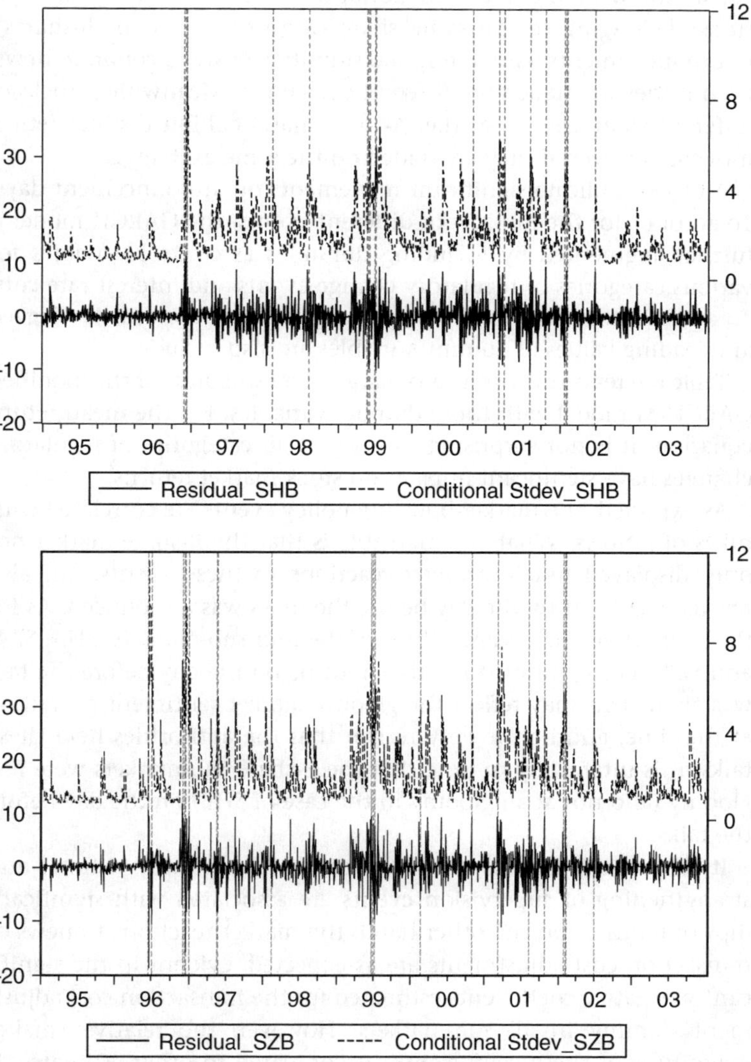

Figure 6.2 Continued

consistent with the standard deviation statistics in Table 6.1. For stocks belonging to the same share category (i.e. A- or B-shares), return movements tend to respond simultaneously to common news, even if they are traded on different exchanges. Meanwhile, stocks of different share categories (i.e. A- or B-share) exhibit distinct return movements even if they are traded on the same exchange.

All these indicate significant movements on announcement days. To account for the impacts of different events, the GARCH model is further augmented by including dummies as control variables for various categories of regulatory change events and interest rate cuts. To account for pre-event or post-event impacts, the one-day lagged and leading values of dummy variables are also included.

Table 6.6 reports the results of parameter estimates for the modified GARCH-M model with those dummy variables. For the mean return equation, it is not surprising to see that all categories of regulatory changes have significant impacts on stock market returns.

As expected, the market-boosting policy events are correlated with hikes of returns. What is remarkable is that the B-share market not only displayed much stronger reactions to these events, but also reacted significantly the day before the news was announced. As for the supportive talks events, three of the four sub-markets, SHA, SZA, and SZB, had significant negative returns on the day before the talk was aired. This may reflect the gloomy market sentiment prevailing at the time, and be the very reason that the authorities held these talks. It is interesting to note that the B-share sub-markets were less gloomy (and not at all gloomy in the case of SHB) on the day before the talks.

It is also interesting to note that the disciplinary actions and strengthening of supervision events are associated with significant dips of returns. On the other hand, the market reactions to news of transaction cost adjustments are as expected, evident in the significantly negative coefficients estimated for the transaction cost adjustment dummy in all sub-markets. However, the relative smaller magnitude of these coefficients, as compared to other estimates, is worthy of note.

Market expansion effects on returns are equally intriguing. When such expansions were for both the A- and B-share markets, the impacts on both categories of sub-markets were significantly negative, as generally expected (by the conventional understanding of demand

Table 6.6 Estimation results of the GARCH (1, 1)-M model (with dummy)

Coefficient	**SHA**	**SZA**	**SHB**	**SZB**
Mean equation				
GARCH	0.0214	0.0271**	0.0259**	0.0102
Constant	−0.0029	−0.0259	−0.1101	−0.0215
D_ Boost(−1)	0.0027	0.1183	1.0577***	0.7508***
D_ Boost	2.1924***	2.5090***	3.8909***	4.3907***
D_ Boost(1)	−0.4044	−0.4380	−0.1710	−0.0482
D_ Disc(−1)	−0.2554	−0.3654	−0.1816	−0.9273**
D_ Disc	−3.3224***	−3.0501***	−3.6648***	−3.3890***
D_ Disc(1)	−0.0897	−0.0931	−0.9418***	−0.4026
D_ supp(−1)	−1.6406***	−2.2691***	−0.6813	−1.5094***
D_ supp	3.6086***	3.7972***	3.0835***	5.3078***
D_ supp(1)	0.2307	0.7152	−0.3806	0.1179
D_ exp1(−1)	−0.7555	−0.3025	−1.6210*	1.1807
D_ exp1	−3.7966***	−3.5464***	3.8493***	2.3731***
D_ exp1(1)	0.3684	0.9230	1.2674	1.9153**
D_ cost(−1)	−0.6458	−0.4028	−0.3106	0.1758
D_ cost	−1.1494**	−1.5938**	−0.8689***	−0.8899***
D_ cost(1)	0.1434	0.1808	−0.3365	−0.2799
D_ exp2(−1)	0.3238	0.2363	−0.5198*	0.0802
D_ exp2	−2.9057***	−2.7349***	−4.1540***	−3.6023***
D_ exp2(1)	0.2328	0.0174	−0.8228	−0.7092
D_ interest(−1)	−0.5495	−0.3378	−0.3190	0.2214
D_ interest	−0.4107	−0.0882	0.1398	0.9943***
D_ interest(1)	0.5092	0.5401	−0.1285	−0.4693
AR(1)/MA(1)	NA	NA	0.0906***	0.1187***
Variance equation				
Constant	0.4478***	0.2845***	0.0576***	0.0502***
ARCH(1)	0.1902***	0.2750***	0.2555***	0.3313***
GARCH(1)	0.7196***	0.6656***	0.7180***	0.6308***
D_ holiday	3.2025***	3.4335***	4.1859***	3.3600***
D_ limit	−0.3546***	−0.1873***	0.0312*	0.1282***

Notes:

(1) ***, ** and * indicates t-value significant at 1%, 5% and 10% level respectively.

(2) D_ Boost = dummy for 'market-boosting policy'; D_ Disc = dummy for 'disciplinary action and strengthening of supervision'; D_ supp = dummy for 'supportive talks by officials and commentary in press'; D_ exp1 = dummy for 'market expansion (for only A- or B-share)'; D_ cost = dummy for 'transaction cost adjustment (stamp duty, commission etc)'; D_ exp2 = dummy for 'market expansion (for both A- and B-shares)'; D_ interest = dummy for 'prime interest rate cut'; D_ holiday = dummy for the day after the long public holiday.

(3) Except for D_cost and D_exp2, all the dummies in (2) are of value 0 or 1, with '1' indicating the occurrence of the event.

(4) In the case of D_cost, the dummy is of value −1, 0, or +1, with '+1' refers to the event of 'transaction cost rise', '−1' refers to the event of 'transaction cost cut', and '0' to 'no-event'.

(5) In the case of D_exp2, the dummy is of value −1, 0, or +1, with '+1' refers to the event of 'market expansion', '0' to no-event, and '−1' refers to the event of 'suspension of the market expansion planned earlier' (e.g. on 23 June, 2002, the State Council called for a stop to the sale of state-controlled shares in listed companies).

(6) D_ limit = dummy with value '1' for all the trading days after the imposition of daily price change limits on 16 December 1996, and '0' otherwise.

and supply). When the expansions were either for only the A-share market or the B-share market, they had opposite impacts on returns of the two types of shares: A-share returns would plunge but B-share returns would rise on their respective market expansion events.

In contrast to significant impacts of regulatory changes, interest rate cuts have the expected significant effects on the SZB market only. The seeming insensitivity of the investors to interest rate changes may be due to the fact that the adjustment rate was generally well anticipated by the market by means of a series of policy debates and discussions.

In the conditional variance equations estimated by the modified GARCH-M model, the coefficients for D_holiday are positive and highly significant for all sub-markets, indicating that stock market volatility is much higher on the first trading day after the long public holiday. The imposition of a 10 per cent limit on the daily price change in December 1996 appeared to have the opposite effect on the return volatility in the A-share market, as compared to that in the B-share market. The significantly negative coefficients for D_limit in the A-share sub-markets suggest that the regulation effectively constrained the volatility after the limit was imposed. Contrarily, in the case of B-share sub-markets, the volatility did not fall but instead rose. This indicates that the daily volatility in the B-share market was generally well within the 10 per cent range limit before its imposition.

Conclusion

In this study, we group the regulatory changes and policy adjustments from 1995–2003 into six major categories, and use a modified ARIMA outlier detection procedure to identify large shifts of market returns in the sub-markets. Estimation of a modified GARCH-M model reveals remarkable asymmetric market reactions to certain categories of events. These results not only provide useful hints for investors, but also indicate some institutional features of China's stock market development.

First, we discover the asymmetric reactions to the events of market-boosting policy and supportive talks between A- and B-share markets. In particular, the B-share market reacted positively a day before the event of market-boosting policy and appeared to be less gloomy before the supportive talk was aired. A most plausible explanation of the different reactions is that many B-share investors might have an information advantage over their A-share counterparts in anticipating such these events. In fact, despite segmentation between the A- and B-share markets, about 80 per cent of the B-share trading volumes were accounted for by indigenous Chinese investors even before the ban on domestic investors' access to B-share trading was lifted in 2001.[12] It is logical to infer that most of these B-share Chinese investors have a higher social status, with better access to governmental inside information.

Second, our results show that investors in all sub-markets reacted negatively to the disciplinary actions and strengthening of supervision events. Since disciplinary actions and strengthening of supervision were supposed to provide better protection for investors' rights, why did markets react so negatively to these events? One possibility is that these regulatory measures were perceived to be insufficient by the investors, who had held higher expectations for prospect of reforms but were disappointed by the announced measures. Another plausible explanation is that, since the trading irregularity is so prevalent in the market, government has to tolerate it in order to maintain market momentum (Heilmann 2002). In such context, regulators' disciplinary actions and strengthening of supervision might damp investors' zeal and cause stock prices to plunge. For instance, before the ban on domestic investors in B-share trading was lifted in 2001, there were cases where regulators' efforts to enforce the ban cause panic selling in the B-share market.

The third remarkable finding is the opposite impacts of market expansion news regarding A- or B-share market on returns of the two types of shares. A possible interpretation of these opposite movements may lie in the fact that, due to the restriction of B-share market access to domestic investors and the close dual-listing substitutes for B-shares in the form of dual listed shares in Hong Kong and other overseas markets, B-shares are usually traded with a discount price as compared to their A-share counterparts (Sun and Tong 2000). Market expansion regarding the B-share market usually allows more companies to be dually listed in both A- and B-share markets, and thus enhances convergence of the prices for the two types of shares. On top of that, since the B-share market was much smaller than the A-share market, its expansion would improve the liquidity of its shares, making them more attractive to investors.

Finally, our estimation of the conditional variance equations reveals that the imposition of a daily price range limit on 16 December, 1996 was actually a breath of fresh air for the B-share market, so that volatility was slightly (and significantly in SBZ) boosted rather than constrained, as happened in the A-share market. A possible explanation may be that the limits on the A-share market had forced some investors to hedge their positions by trading more actively in the B-share market. Another possibility is that the return of Hong Kong to China in July 1997 made the B-share market more accessible to domestic investors, so that B-share trading became more active and volatile in the subsequent years.

Notes

1. Whether and to what extent the two sub-markets of China's stock exchanges are segmented/integrated has attracted much attention in the literature. See Yang (2003) for recent evidence of segmentation.
2. On 19 February 2001, the Chinese Securities Regulatory Commission announced that Chinese citizens would be allowed to own B-share stocks traded on both the Shanghai and Shenzhen Stock Exchanges. Even after this regulatory change, B-share trading is still not freely accessible to most Chinese indigenous investors since Chinese currency Renminbi is still not convertible for capital account transactions.
3. Inclusion of *China Securities Bulletin* into the event source makes it possible to record market rumours about possible regulatory changes and political events, that do not usually appear in official media of Mainland China. Interviews with some Chinese domestic equity analysts and investors confirm that such information is generally accessible to domestic investors through the brokerage companies.
4. The period is determined partially because the *People's Daily* online database provides information from the beginning of 1995. Besides, before 1995, there were only a few listed companies and the stock market indices were dominated by one or two largest companies.
5. Due to space limit, detail records of the event days and their contents are not included in this chapter but are available upon request. Here 'event day' refer to the day that information is made public. When the information was issued after the trading hours of stock exchanges or occurred during the weekend or other non-trading days, the following trading day would be referred.
6. We also tried a less sophisticated approach of Cutler *et al.* (1999) to match the largest daily market movements to their 'causes'. The results of that approach are similar to that of modified outlier identification procedure. The advantage of using the latter procedure is its ability to identify level shifts and trend in stock market movements.

7. All the four index returns are of integration of order one. There is a AR(1) item for the SHB return and a MA(1) item for the SZB return. No AR or MA item is found for SHA and SZA return time series.
8. The percentages for all 'causes' categories may add up to more than 100 per cent since certain dates are coded under multiple 'causes'. Due to space limit, full records of the outlier return days and their associated events are not listed but are available upon request.
9. The non-domestic events include NATO's bombing of the Chinese embassy in Yugoslavia and the escalating tensions in Taiwan Straits.
10. Similarly, Kutan and Yuan (2003) found no impact of key macroeconomic new release on China's stock market.
11. In the ARIMA model estimated in the last section we find returns in SHB (SZB) are best fitted with autocorrelation (moving average) item of order one, so an AR (MA) of order 1 with GARCH (1, 1)-M model is estimated for SHB (SZB).
12. 'Beijing Opens Class-B Shares to Local Chinese Investors', *Asian Wall Street Journal*, 20 February 2001.

References

Chan, Yue-cheong and Wei, K.C. John (1996) 'Political Risk and Stock Price Volatility: The Case of Hong Kong', *Pacific-Basin Finance Journal*, 4, 259–75.

Cutler, David M., Poterva, James M. and Summers, Lawrence H. (1989) 'What Moves the Stock Prices?', *Journal of Portfolio Management*, 15(3), 4–12.

Edmonds, Radcliffe and Kutan, Ali M. (2002) 'Is the Public Information Really Relevant in Asset Markets?', *Economic Letters*, 76(3), 223–9.

Gao, Y. and Tse, Y.K. (2001) 'Capital Control, Market Segmentation and Cross-border Flow of Information: Some Empirical Evidence from the Chinese Stock Market', Working paper, Singapore Management University.

Heilmann, Sebastian (2002) 'The Chinese Stock Market: Pitfalls of a Policy-drive Market', Working paper, Centre for East Asian and Pacific Studies, Trier University, Germany.

Jones, C. and Seguin, P. (1997) 'Transaction Cost and Price Volatility: Evidence from the Commission Deregulation', *American Economic Review*, 87(4), 728–37.

Karolyi, A.G. and Li, L. (2003) 'A Resolution of the Chinese Discount Puzzle', Working paper, Ohio State University.

Kim, Harold Y. and Mei, Jianping P. (2001) 'What Makes the Stock Market Jump? An Analysis of Political Risk on Hong Kong Stock Returns', *Journal of International Money and Finance*, 20, 1003–16.

Kutan, Ali M. and Yuan, Shangkuan (2003) 'Does Public Information Arrival Matter in Emerging Markets? Evidence from Stock Exchanges in China', Working paper, Southern Illinois University.

Lo, W.C. and Chan, W.S. (2000) 'Diagnosing Shocks in Stock Market Returns of Greater China', *Multinational Finance Journal*, 4, 269–99.

Ma, Xianghai (1996) 'Capital Controls, Market Segmentation and Stock Prices: Evidence from the Chinese Stock Market', *Pacific-Basin Finance Journal*, 4, 219–39.

Nelson, D. (1991) 'Conditional Heteroscedasticity in Asset Returns: A New Approach', *Econometrica*, 59, 347–71.
Su, Dongwei and Fleisher, Belton M. (1998) 'Risk, Return and Regulation in Chinese Stock Markets', *Journal of Economics and Business*, 50, 239–56.
Sun, Q. and Tong, W.H.S. (2000) 'The Effect of Market Segmentation on Stock Prices: The China Syndrome', *Journal of Banking and Finance*, 24, 1875–1902.
Umlauf, S.R. (1993) 'Transaction Taxes and the Behaviour of the Swedish Stock Market', *Journal of Financial Economics*, 33, 227–40.
Vandaele, W. (1983) *Applied Time Series and Box–Jenkins Models* (Orlando: Academic Press).
Walter, Carl E. and Howie, Fraser J.T. (2001) *To Get Rich is Glorious: China's Stock Markets in the 80s and 90s* (London: Palgrave).
Xu, Cheng Kenneth (2000) 'The Microstructure of the Chinese Stock Market', *China Economy Review*, 11, 79–97.
Yang, Jian (2003) 'Market Segmentation and Information Asymmetry in Chinese Stock Markets: A VAR Analysis', *Financial Review*, 38, 591–610.

7
Technical Trading Strategies and Market Efficiency

Robert Ślepaczuk

Introduction

The subject of market efficiency is widely analyzed by finance theorists keen to discover whether it is possible to create an investment strategy that can generate abnormal returns on the basis of given information Φ_t. If capital markets are efficient, then shares and other financial instruments can be quoted at proper prices and reflect the value of assets adequately and fairly, and no abnormal profits can be made. This concept is directly related to the efficient market hypothesis (EMH), which can be presented in three forms, depending on the set of available information Φ_t at time t. The opposite view is that the price of financial instruments contain systematic and discoverable mistakes, and investors who notice those deviations can succeed in obtaining abnormal profits.

Information efficiency of capital markets is also connected to the allocation efficiency of the market. Capital markets also reflect how opinions may be formed on future events, such as the possibility of success or failure of investments, project completion, and development of new technologies or demand for particular products. If markets are efficient and prices of financial assets fully reflect investors' expectations, then managers can use those price signals as important tools in their decision making to maximize the value and performance of their companies. On the other hand, if asset prices contain significant and systematic miscalculations, then managers' plans can fail due to divergence between correct and incorrect prices.

The basic purpose of the present study is to verify the weak form information efficiency of derivatives quoted on the Warsaw Stock

Exchange (WSE). The study also contains analyses of reasons for differences in the information efficiency of various instruments, and draws some conclusions regarding the range of optimum parameters of certain investment strategies.

The study has some unique features. First, it focuses on tests of weak form information efficiency of the market that are based on buy/sell signals used in technical analysis (TA). Second, it presents a very new element in studies on EMH, as it is conducted on the futures market rather than the spot market. The use of the futures market has made it possible to consider not only the buy transactions, but also the sell transactions of financial instruments. Indeed, contrary to the short sell transactions that were not possible on the spot market, here it was possible to allow for the long sale of futures contracts during the test period. This approach made the conditions under research similar to real life situations in well developed capital markets. The next new element was the procedure of optimization of investment strategies based on individual buy/sell signals. All these new elements allowed the market efficiency hypothesis to be considered from a different point of view. The next two sections provide some background information on the research and some of the tests carried out on capital market efficiency. Explanations are given for the assumptions and description of the tests carried out in the study, and the subsequent section explains the nine different investment strategies that are constructed on the basis of technical analysis and optimized. The criteria used in selection of particular derivatives in this study are then given and the results of the tests presented. The remainder of the chapter reports on the implications of the results for EMH and some of the possible reasons for deviations from it.

Capital market efficiency

EMH is believed to be one of the most important concepts in the theory of finance. A capital market is considered to be informationally efficient when information is rapidly transferred to all market participants, and security prices fully and immediately reflect all the information. Hence, financial instruments are always fairly priced.[1]

The theory of capital market efficiency is based on Fama (1970), which was in fact first defined by Roberts (1959).[2] According to the theory, an efficient market fully reflects the set of information Φ_t. Fama

(1970)[3] defined three forms of EMH based on three different levels of information that are reflected in securities prices. Weak-form EMH states that rates of return should reflect all the information implied in historical price quotations (i.e. prices include the set of information Φ_I). Semi-strong form EMH states that price quotations should reflect all past and present information publicly available, (prices include set of information Φ_{II}). That is, not only the information readable from the time series of stock prices, but also the wide range of details presented in financial statements of companies, and other announced information that affects stock prices. Strong-form EMH states that a market is extremely efficient when all sorts of information are mirrored in stock prices. In this case, both widely available and confidential information are taken into consideration (set of information Φ_{III}).

The above definitions assume that fluctuations in prices of financial assets are random because prices always reflect a given set of information. In other words, prices are always informationally efficient. If the market is informationally efficient in the weak form, then technical analysis based on charts of past quoted prices is not beneficial. Strictly speaking, it is not possible to use technical analysis based on price charts to create an investment strategy that can generate abnormal gains.

If the semi-strong form of EMH holds, then none of the analyses that use the widely available information can produce more profitable rates of return than the market averages. Based on this hypothesis, fundamental analysis has no use in practice. Finally, if the market shows the strong form of EMH, then any efforts to gather information to generate abnormal profit is pointless. Market traders who have access to confidential information will not achieve any advantage over the others as the prices of financial instruments have already included all such information.

Bearing in mind the above assumptions, the set of information determining weak-form EMH is included in the set of information determining semi-strong form EMH, and those in turn are included in the set of information determining strong-form EMH. In other words:

$$\Phi_I \subset \Phi_{II} \subset \Phi_{III}$$

Thus, strong-form efficiency encompasses the condition for semi-strong form efficiency, and that in turn encompasses the condition for weak-form efficiency. The above relations have a significant implication for the results of this study, which tries to verify the application of weak-form EMH in the Warsaw Stock market.

One might argue that the empirical assessment of EMH is more interesting than the mere theoretical argument of the hypothesis. The question of what is the most appropriate theory in practice has raised a number of questions, and analysts are constantly trying to find the reasons why EMH should hold, and which one of the three forms is valid in reality. These questions might be approached in different ways. First, one might try to discover whether it is possible to design an investment strategy that allows the gain of higher than average returns in the long term. Knowledge concerning the level of market efficiency that might hold in reality is beneficial in this case. That is because such knowledge can enable investors to design an investment strategy that uses the set of information that is most appropriate for a 'beat the market' strategy. Second, this knowledge might allow managers to predict market response to their decisions, and hence affect the company's management and policy.

Surveys verifying market efficiency hypotheses

A great deal of research to verify market efficiency hypotheses has been carried out since 1970s, following the publication of Fama (1970). Unfortunately, conclusions that were drawn from those studies could not be demonstrated transparently and coherently. In spite of ambiguity in the results of many of the studies, it is fair to say that while the financial society has mostly rejected the validity of the strong-form EMH, it has generally accepted that of the weak-form EMH, without giving much recognition or credibility to technical analysis. The approach to semi-strong form EMH, however, still remains controversial, especially among investors who try to take advantage of fundamental analysis.[4]

The following is a summary of the findings of some of the most important studies that proved exceptions to the theory.

Strong-form efficiency

The majority of studies found that strong-form EMH is not a useful or accurate description of reality. Confidential information cannot be included in prices if it has not been announced to the market by well-informed investors' transactions or announced to the public in some other way. Tests of strong-form EMH were conducted on the average rate of return of institutional investors on the assumption that they had access to confidential information. The results were then compared with the market averages, such as the average rate of return of S&P index in the case of American markets. One example of such studies is Jaffe (1974), which was based on the use of confidential information by investors before announcements of stock split, increase in dividends and mergers of the companies. This study proved that it is possible to take advantage of confidential information and obtain abnormal gains. There are other studies such as Friend *et al.* (1962), and Cornell and Roll (1981), which offer similar results and hence reject the strong form of EMH.

There are also studies such as Jensen (1969) and Czekaj, Woś, Żarnowski (2001) on the Polish market that opt to support the strong form of market efficiency. From a methodological point of view, strong-form EMH is the most difficult form to examine due to problems of verification of the flow of confidential information.

Semi-strong form efficiency

In the case of tests of semi-strong form EMH, only imprecise conclusions could be drawn. Occasionally, there are some studies that argue against the semi-strong form of EMH. Practical examples, however, are more in favour of the semi-strong form of EMH, and tend to suggest that prices adjust immediately to publicized information, thus making it impossible to make use of hints coming from fundamental analysis. Some of the most interesting studies that have examined the semi-strong form of EMH are the following:

- Fama, French, Jensen and Roll (1969) examined the effect of share split on security prices and increase in dividends, and confirmed that the semi-strong form of EMH holds.
- Kraus and Stoll (1972), tested the reaction of prices to new offerings of stocks and found an immediate price walk to the previous value of stocks, which proved market efficiency.
- Basu (1977) assessed the influence of the price earnings ratio (P/E) on the rate of return, and found that stocks with a lower P/E tend to have a higher risk weighted rate of return compared with stocks with a higher P/E. Similarly Banz (1981) revealed that the rate of

return is higher in the case of companies with a lower rate of capitalization. Based on their results, both studies rejected the semi-strong form of EMH.

- Czekaj, Woś and Żarnowski (2001) tested the outcome of strategies based on analysis of P/E ratio, the capitalization effect and the *P/BV* ratio (price to book value ratio) effect for the Polish capital market between September 1994 and September 2000. Their study proved the efficiency of the capital market with no significant increase in the rate of return.

Weak-form efficiency

Another group of anomalies was shown by studies that did not confirm weak-form EMH. They were mainly related to the following calendar effects: month-of-the year, week-of-the month, day-of-the week and hour-of-the day.[5] Each of above effects weakened the validity of weak-form EMH, though their seasonality and changes over time reduced their credibility.

One of the most popular effects is the January effect. Rozeff and Kinney (1976) showed that the average rate of return on the NYSE in January is significantly higher than the rate of return in other months. Keim (1983) showed the combination of the January effect and low capitalization affected the companies' rate of return, with the former being responsible in nearly half of changes in the annual rate of return. Ariel (1987) conducted a study on the week-of-the month effect using data from 1963 to 1981. He divided the month into two equal halves and discovered that the cumulated rate of return for the first half of the month during the 19 years equalled 2552 per cent, while for the second half equalled nearly zero per cent. On the other hand, French (1980) checked the days-of-the-week effect and found that while the average rate of return on Mondays was negative, that of other days of the week was positive. The last example is Harris (1986), which looked at the effect of the shortest period of time on prices and found that prices generally showed some tendency to decrease during the first 45 minutes of trading on Mondays, but appeared to increase during the other days of the week.

All these studies showed anomalies that indicated periodical deviations from the EMH. Even if one attaches a low weight to the significance of studies related to the effect of the shortest periods, it is still difficult to refute the significance of the January effect, which seems to be the strongest evidence against the weak-form EMH.

A few years ago, Czekaj, Woś, Żarnowski (2001) used certain concepts of technical analysis to verify the validity of weak-form EMH in the Polish capital market between the years 1994–2000. They used signals generated by moving averages and oscillators, and found that the tools used did not help in gaining abnormal rates of return. However, their assumptions will be examined later in this chapter.

Before proceeding further, let us specify some of the assumptions of the random walk tests used in financial literature together with technical analysis (TA) investment strategies tests to verify weak-form EMH. A market is weak-form efficient when the historical prices follow the random walk process. In other words, a market is said to be informationally efficient when market prices are independent of each other. The following tests (not conducted in this chapter) can be used to verify the above characteristics:

Autocorrelation tests of independence

The objective of this test is to check the size of the correlation coefficient between the price changes in periods t and $t = s$:[6]

$$\rho_{t,t-s} = cor(\Delta y_t, \Delta y_{t-s}) \tag{7.1}$$

where y_t is the price in the period t, and y_{t-s} is the price in period $t-s$.

For a market to be characterized by weak form efficiency, the correlation coefficient between the changes of the prices ought to be zero or close to zero, i.e.

$$\rho_{t,t-s} \in (-\ 0.1, 0.1) \tag{7.2}$$

Runs tests

These are popular statistical tests that are used to verify whether the sequences of upward and downward movements of the prices follow the random walk. If we can prove this, we can confirm the weak-form EMH. In runs tests, the number of sequences of consecutive positive and negative returns, or runs, is tabulated and compared against its sampling distribution under the random walk hypothesis.

Tests of distribution of the rate of returns

Here the hypothesis (H_0) that the data is generated in a random walk process will be tested. If H_0 is true, then there should be a linear dependence between the variance and the period of time during which the variance is measured.

The relevant formulas for tests presented above can be found, for example, in Campbell, Lo and MacKinley (1997).

In the 1980s and 1990s, many anomalies were observed that proved that rates of return are not randomly distributed. The emergence of those anomalies in practice contradicted the validity of EMH. Obviously, by definition anomalies are short-term deviations from the norm. Nevertheless, their occurrence should be noted as an indication of possibility of exceptions to the rules, which might be repeated in the future, and hence should be considered more seriously in the theory.

Test assumptions

As mentioned earlier the basic objective of the present study is to verify the weak form of EMH in the case of futures contracts and the index participation unit on the Warsaw Stock Exchange (WSE), with conditions similar to those that exist in the market.

The examination of capital market efficiency was conducted in few stages. In the first stage, nine different investment strategies that are commonly used in Technical Analysis (TA) were identified, (the feature of each strategy is explained in more detail on pp. 101–10). In each case, the parameters (parameters of the strategy are, for example, the length of the period for short-term and long-term moving averages, or the type of the moving averages) of those strategies were optimized on the basis of historical data of particular financial instruments. Next, the daily and weekly percentage rates of return on investments were calculated for the optimized strategies on the basis of two methods of calculation of the initial investment on the futures contracts. These are the following:

- the initial investment is considered to be equal to the initial deposit of the investor at the moment of taking position. This allows the effect of financial leverage to be taken into account which causes the rates of returns from tested strategies to be higher and show a larger standard deviation.

- the initial investment is considered to be equal to the contract value, which equals the contract price multiplied by the multiplier. Multipliers for each future contracts being tested in this chapter are presented in Table 7.1 (p. 111).

In the first stage of the study, 15 listed derivatives quoted on the WSE were used for the tests. These fall under the following four categories:

- Index futures contracts: WIG20 (Warsaw Stock Exchange WIG20 Index), TECHWIG (Index for SiTech Segment TechWIG), MIDWIG (Warsaw Stock Exchange Mid Cap Index MIDWIG)
- Currency futures contracts: EUR/PLN (Euro/Polish Zloty) and USD/PLN (US dollar/Polish Zloty)
- Equity futures contracts for nine stocks: AGORA SA, BANK BPH SA, BRE BANK SA, ELEKTRIM SA, KGHM POLSKA MIEDZ SA, BANK POLSKA KASA OPIEKI SA, PROKOM SOFTWARE SA, POLSKI KONCERN NAFTOWY ORLEN SA, TELEKOMUNIKACJA POLSKA SA
- Index participation units on the Warsaw Stock Exchange WIG20 Index.

In selecting the derivatives, both maximization of the number of tested contracts and periods of quotation on the market were taken into account.

Optimization tests for particular derivatives were conducted, using the available data from the beginning of their quotation on the market until 11 July 2003. In each case a buy and hold strategy (the control strategy) was devised, where it was assumed that a given stock was purchased on the first day of quotation and held up to the last day (i.e. the day of the test, which was 11 July 2003). The rate of return of this strategy is the difference between the closing price on the last day and the first day of quotation divided by the closing price on the first day. The rates of return for buy and hold strategies were calculated using the same sample of data as that of the technical analysis strategy. These rates of return were then used as the basis for comparison of the buy and hold strategy with tested strategies of technical analysis.

Futures contracts have a specified term to reach maturity (nine months from the first day of quotation for each of the series). In order to test various strategies for the contracts, it was necessary to use continuous charts. These were created by replacing series of expiring quotations with series of the earliest date of maturity. This procedure made available series of data from the first day of quotation for each type of futures contract. Optimization tests were then conducted on daily data, and signals were generated on the basis of closing prices of continuous charts.

In order to construct particular indicators of technical analysis, daily data on closing price, opening price, high price, low price, volume and open interest were tested. The tests included the transaction costs of buying and selling securities. The average commission was assumed to be 20 PLN per opening or closing position, which nowadays constitutes a compromise between higher transaction costs in the past and lower costs.

All the tested TA strategies were continuous strategies (i.e. after generating the first buy/sell signal, there was continuous active trading with buy or sell signals). In addition, it was assumed that only one contract could be opened at any moment. If a long position[7] was taken and a buy signal had been generated, then two short positions were taken, which eventually resulted in only one active short position.[8]

Transactions were made on the closing price of each day after buy/sell signals were generated. It was assumed that the closing prices could be approximated at the level where a signal was generated. This assumption was not incompatible with market reality, and allowed the creation of conditions similar to the real world. In practice, it enhanced the reliability of results, and helped to draw interesting conclusions.

Technical analysis tools used in generating buy/sell signals

The techniques used in technical analysis are all based on historical prices. Therefore, strategies that are based on those prices were considered appropriate for testing the weak-form efficiency hypothesis. The nine different investment strategies that were selected were the most popular in a wide range of techniques used in technical analysis, and considered to be the most suitable for investment in practice.

Each strategy was based on buy/sell signals used in technical analysis. Next, MetaStock Professional, version 8.0 – a software used in stock analyses – was used to optimize the volumes and parameters of each strategy (specified in detail below). The aim of the optimization tests was to find the best set of parameters that could be used in technical analysis to define buy/sell signals in investment strategies. All combinations of parameters (presented in detail below the strategy descriptions) were tests to determine the best combination of parameters for each investment strategy that could generate the highest profit during the tested period. The strategies used were as follows:

Strategy 1 Moving average (MA)

The first strategy was based on the moving average, which is one of the most universal and popular techniques used in technical analysis because it does not involve any subjective assessment of the situation under consideration, as is common in many other methods. MA is used in a vast majority of technical analysis because of the ease of its construction and the fact that it does not require complicated calculation and verification.

The moving average is defined as the average of a given set of data which moves on over time. For example, in an n-day average, prices of the last n-days should be summed up and divided by n. The term 'moving', then, implies that every time a new price is added to the series and the number of observation rises to $n + 1$, the first closing price will be subtracted from the series and only the last n-days will be taken into account in calculation of the average of n days of data. Consequently, the average of n days keeps changing, and only the average closing price of the last n-days of trading will be considered.

The moving average usually follows the trend and can be treated as its curve. Therefore, it is usually applied either to identify current trends or to foresee new emerging trends. It can be calculated in many different ways. In building strategy I and indirectly modelling the other strategies, the following types of MA were used:

Simple moving average (S) is an ordinary arithmetic average which is often used in the construction of various indicators in technical analysis:

$$S_n = \frac{\sum_{i=1}^{n} C_{i-1}}{n} \tag{7.3}$$

where

S_n is *n*-days simple moving average,

C_{i-1} is the closing price $i-1$ days ago, with i varying from 1 to *n*,

n is the number of periods used to count the moving average.

Weighted moving average (W) is weighted moving average. In order to calculate this the greatest weight is allocated to the last closing prices and the lowest weight to the historical ones:

$$W_n = \frac{\sum_{i=1}^{n} (n - i + 1) * C_{i-1}}{\frac{(n+1) * n}{2}} \tag{7.4}$$

where

W_n is the weighted moving average at time *n*,

C_{i-1} is the closing price $i-1$ days ago, with i varying from 1 to *n*.

Exponential moving average (E) is a moving average that allocates a larger weight to more recent prices, and hence, in that sense, it is a form of weighted average. However, by attaching lower weights to past prices, it includes all the data related to the historical prices of a given stock. In this method, current prices can be assigned a minor or major weight. This can be achieved by assigning a certain percentage value to the closing price of the previous day, that will then be added to the percentage value of the exponential moving average of the previous day:

$$E_n = \alpha * C_0 + (1 - \alpha) * E_n^{-1} \tag{7.5}$$

$$\alpha = 2/(n + 1) \tag{7.6}$$

where

E_n is *n* periods exponential moving average. This average is calculated today on the basis of the last *n* closing prices (i.e. C_0, C_1, C_2, ..., C_{n-1}),

E_n^{-1} is the previous value of *n*-periods *E*,

α is the exponential percentage.

Time periods moving average (T) is calculated on the basis of the linear regression method. Instead of marking the linear regression line on the price chart, only the average of the last points included in the line will be considered on the basis of the closing prices of n days. For the subsequent regression lines, these points would be tied on a curve which forms a moving average time series chart.[9]

Volume adjusted moving average (VOL) is similar to the method weighted moving average uses, defined as a system of analyzed variable weighting. The most important element in this method is the days with the highest volume values:[10]

$$VOL_n = \sum_{i=1}^{n} \frac{V_{i-1}}{V} * C_{i-1} \tag{7.7}$$

where

V is the sum of the volume from the last n days,

$V_{i\text{-}1}$ is the volume i-days ago.

Variable moving average (VAR) is an exponential moving average that adjusts the number of periods according to the current market volatility. If the volatility increases, then higher weights will be assigned to the closing prices of the previous periods, thus creating a higher exponential percentage in the calculation of the average:

$$\mathrm{VAR_n} = (\alpha * (IZ) * C_0) + (1 - \alpha * IZ) * VAR_{\mathrm{n}}^{-1} \tag{7.8}$$

where

$\mathrm{VAR_n^{-1}}$ is the previous value of n periods VAR,

IZ is the volatility index.

Chande's 9-periods impetus oscillator was used to calculate the volatility index in conducted tests.

Triangular moving average (TRI) is similar to the weighted and exponential average. The only difference here is that the highest weight will be attached to the closing prices in the first half of the period.

For even n: $x = n/2 + 1/2$

$$\mathrm{TRI_n} = \frac{1}{x}\left[\sum_{i=1}^{x}\left(\frac{1}{x}\sum_{k=1}^{x} C_{(i-1)+(k-1)}\right)\right] \tag{7.9}$$

For uneven n: $y = n/2$

$$\mathrm{TRI_n} = \frac{1}{y}\left[\sum_{i=1}^{y}\left(\frac{1}{y+1}\sum_{k=1}^{y+1} C_{(i-1)+(k-1)}\right)\right] \tag{7.10}$$

where TRI_n is the Triangular moving average at time *n*.

In constructing strategy I, the method of crossover moving averages was used. In this method, a buy signal emerges when the short-term average crosses the long-term average from below and a sell signal appears when the short term average crosses the long term average from above. Short-term and long-term refers to the number of periods used to calculate the moving averages. This is a continuous strategy, as there is always an open position in the market.

In this strategy, parameters of all the above seven moving averages were optimized. The process of optimization allows the determination of the period of short-term and long-term averages (OPT1 and OPT2 respectively). It also determines the specific type of moving average (E, S, T, TRI, VAR, VOL, WMA)[11] that generates the best results (measured in terms of total profit) on the basis of historical prices. The OPT1 and OPT2 parameters were determined through the process of optimization of daily data on closing prices, using a set ranging from 1 to 100 periods in every single period. In other words, every combination of periods (ranging from 1 to 100 days for short- and long-term) which is used to calculate moving average was checked in the optimization process to find the best set of those parameters when we consider the total profit from the investment strategy point of view.

Strategy 2 Bollinger bands (BB)

This method was described by John Bollinger. The most important characteristic of this method is that two bands are placed around the n-days average (Bollinger bands). The distance of each band from the average is two (or more) standard deviations.[12] The two standard deviations band on each side allow for 95 per cent of the price data to be included between the two bands. If prices reach the area above the upper band or below the lower band, then it means that price volatility or impetus[13] (i.e. the speed of price change) reaches its extreme values and the market becomes overbought or oversold. An overbought condition occurs when the oscillators reach the upper extreme values and the market rises too much. In such cases, the probability of a rise in supply and fall in prices goes up. An oversold condition, on the other hand, arises when the oscillator reaches the lower extreme, and the market drops too far. This time the probability of a rise in price increases significantly (see Murphy 1999).

A buy signal appears when the closing prices enter the oversold area and reappears in the area between the two bands. A long position closing signal arises when closing prices cross the upper-band in a given day. A sell signal becomes visible when prices are above the upper band and then return to the area between the two bands. Accordingly, the entry of prices below the lower band area imply a short-term position signal.

Under these tactics, the following were optimized: parameters related to the type of average (E, S, T, TRI, VAR, W), the length of period of the average (OPT1: ranging from 1 to 100 in each period) and the number of standard deviations determining the distance of the band from the average (OPT 2: ranging from 1 to 7 in each period).

Strategy 3 Commodity Channel Index (CCI)

The next investment strategy was based on the Commodity Channel Index formula defined by Donald Lambert. CCI formula[14] determines the figure that statistically expresses the distance of prices from the moving average. If the distance is sufficient (sufficiency depends on the number of periods, the oversold and overbought level, etc.), it is assumed that the trend is already shaped and this is considered to be the buy/sell signal.

The process of computation of this indicator is as follows:
We compute current typical price (X_1) making the use of high price (H), low price (L) and closing price (C):

$$X_1 = \frac{H + L + C}{3} \tag{7.11}$$

Next, we compute the moving average for n-previous typical prices:

$$\overline{X} = \frac{1}{n}\sum_{i=1}^{n} X_i \tag{7.12}$$

Then, we compute the median deviation (MD) for n-previous typical prices:

$$MD = \frac{1}{n}\sum_{i=1}^{n} |X_i - \overline{X}| \tag{7.13}$$

We calculate CCI:

$$CCI = \frac{1.5 * (X_i - \overline{X})}{MD} \tag{7.14}$$

In order to apply the CCI indicator, one needs to specify the oversold and overbought areas (such as + and −100 respectively) for which the buy/sell signals can be defined. In this strategy, the buy signal, which is also the signal for short closing price position, will appear when the CCI indicator is below −100, and then the closing price rises above the −100 level. The sell signal, on the other hand, which is the same as a long position closing signal, appears when prices exceed +100 level and then fall below that level.

Under this strategy, the number of periods for which the CCI indicator is computed (OPT1: ranging from 1 to 50 in each period and the level of oversold and overbought areas) were optimized (OPT2: ranging from 100 to 300 every twentieth period in the case of an overbought area and similarly with a minus sign for an oversold area).

Strategy 4 Moving average penetration

In the MA penetration strategy, once again the concept of a moving average is used. Here, a buy signal is generated at the moment when the closing price of a given day exceeds the value of the moving average. A sell signal, on the other hand, is generated when the closing price of a given day falls below the moving average.

Under this strategy, parameters of moving averages were optimized in order to determine the following:

- The best MA method among the seven types (i.e. E, S, T, TRI, VAR, VOL, W)
- The best length of periods for which the average had to be calculated (OPT2: ranging from 1 to 200 days in each period).

Strategy 5 Directional Movement Index (DMI)

In the fifth strategy, the concept of directional movement was used to calculate one of the most popular indicators of technical analysis; namely, the ADX (Average Directional Index). DMI is an efficient indicator of trend direction. It assumes that in a bullish trend, the current high price should be above that of the previous day and, in a bearish trend, the current low price should be below that of the previous day's minimum. Here, both the positive directional movement (+DM) and negative directional movement (−DM) were calculated to determine the strength of upward and downward trends.

The buy signal appears when +DMI exceeds −DMI, and the sell signal appears when +DMI drops below −DMI.

The purpose of the optimization procedure here is to find the optimal number of periods for calculating the average value of +DMI and −DMI (OPT1: ranging from 1 to 200 in each period).

Strategy 6 Moving average convergence/divergence (MAC/D)

The next investment strategy is based on the MAC/D technique that was first defined by Gerard Appel (1985). MAC/D is an indicator presenting the difference between two exponential moving averages (12 and 26 periods). At any point, the position of the above indicator will be compared with the position of a signal line which is determined by 9 days averages. (In testing, all the parameters (the number of periods for moving averages) were optimized, including the 7 types of moving averages). This process generates an oscillator that produces the buy signal the moment the indicator moves above the signal line and a sell signal when the signal line crosses the chart of the indicator. The MAC/D indicator has gained considerable popularity due to its flexibility, and is used both to determine investments whether there is a trend or not.

Here, a typical MAC/D indicator is defined as 12-26-9, where the difference between the 12- and 26-day averages are calculated, and the signal line is determined by the 9-day average:

$$\text{MAC/D} = E_{12} - E_{26} \tag{7.15}$$

$$\text{Signal line} = E_9 \text{ z MAC/D} \tag{7.16}$$

where

E_{12} is the 12-periods exponential moving average

Under this strategy the following items were optimized:

- The number of periods for the first exponential moving average (OPT1: ranging from 1 to 40 every fourth period)

- The number of periods for the second exponential moving average (OPT2: ranging from 1 to 40 every fourth period)
- The number of periods for signal line (OPT3: ranging from 1 to 20 every second period), the type of calculated average (E, S, T, TRI, VAR, VOL, W).

Strategy 7 Negative Volume Index (NVI)

In this strategy, investors take advantage of the concept of the Negative Volume Index indicator, which focuses on the days in which the volume decreases in comparison to the previous day. This technique is based on the assumption that on the days when the volume is high, there is an 'uninformed crowd' trading on the market. On the days when the volume is low, however, the 'uninformed crowd' is replaced by 'skilled investors'. Therefore, the NVI shows the behaviour of 'wise money'.

The average NVI indicator can also be used as the signal line. Thus, a buy signal is generated the moment NVI crosses the value of its average, and a sell signal is generated when NVI falls below its average.

Under this strategy the following parameters were optimized:

- The number of periods for calculation of the average of NVI (OPT1: ranging from 1 to 200 every second period)
- The type of moving average (E, S, T, TRI, VAR, VOL, W) that was used in the calculation of the NVI.

Strategy 8 Relative Strength Index (RSI)

This strategy was created on the basis of the Relative Strength index, which was provided by Welles Wilder (1978) in order to correct some of the factors that caused imperfections in impetus oscillator, such as misleading signals, lack of uniform scale, and where oversold and overbought areas were different for a given financial instrument. RSI includes an internal smoothing mechanism that allows the reduction of the influence of extreme prices, and creates a fixed scale of RSI ranging from 0 to 100.

In computing RSI, the average of the upward movement of prices (increase in impetus) is compared with the average of downward movement (decrease in impetus) in a given period. Wilder (1978) assumed that in the case of a 14-day period RSI, the overbought and oversold levels were represented by index numbers at 70 and 30[15] respectively.

$$RSI = 100 - [100/(1 + RS)] \tag{7.17}$$

where RS relative strength

The buy signal in this strategy is generated where the closing price falls in the oversold area, and increases above that level thereafter. The sell signal, on the other hand, appears at the moment when a price enters into the overbought area and drops below that level thereafter. Under these tactics, the two parameters that were optimized were the period for RSI calculation (OPT1: ranging from 1 to 50 every single period), and the level of overbought and oversold areas (OPT2: ranging from 2 to 50 every single period for the oversold area and similarly from 50 to 98 every single period for the overbought area).

Strategy 9 Stochastic oscillator

The last investment strategy was created on the basis of a stochastic oscillator. This is a smoothed normalized impetus indicator with a bottom limit of 0 and an upper limit of 100. This oscillator, popularized by George Lane (1986), consists of two lines: %K of the current closing price position in the range of prices defined by the user, and %D of 3-day average of %K which is used as signal line. The signal of possible trend change is generated when %K crosses %D.

The detailed computation of the stochastic oscillator is as follows:

$$\%K = 100 * [(C_0 - L_n)/(H_n - L_n)] \tag{7.18}$$

$$\%D = \text{3-period moving average of } \%K \tag{7.19}$$

where:

C_0 is the present closing price,

H_n is the maximum price from the previous n-days,

L_n is the minimum price from the previous n-days.

The term %D represents a fast oscillator. In most computer programs it is applied in the smoothed version, called a slow stochastic oscillator. The original line %D becomes the new line %K when it is smoothed by 3-day moving average, to create a new slow line %D. Additional smoothing of the slow version decreases the number of failed signals %K%D and also slows down the reaction of oscillator.

Based on this strategy, the following parameters were optimized:

- The level of overbought and oversold areas (OPT1: ranging from 5 to 50 every fifth period for oversold areas and analogically from 50 to 95 every fifth period for overbought areas)
- The number of periods for %K (OPT2: ranging from 2 to 20 every second period)
- The number of periods for %D (OPT3: ranging from 1 to 10 in each period).

The criteria of selection of particular derivatives for survey

The basic purpose of this study was to verify the presence of weak-form EMH in the derivatives market on the Warsaw Stock Exchange (WSE). Among the derivatives listed on the Warsaw Stock Market, the following were chosen: index, equity and currency futures contracts and index participation units on WIG20. Due to the low volume of turnover, optional warrants were excluded.

Also the two futures contracts on Bank Millennium S.A. stocks and Bank Zachodni WBK SA were excluded owing to an insufficient period of their quotation on the WSE (approximately 70 daily data).

The detailed list of derivatives and their description of issues are provided in Table 7.1.

Results

At the beginning of the study, complete tests were conducted on four representative instruments from every group (listed in detail on p. 99). Maximum average daily volume of contract was one of the criteria used in the selection of futures contracts. Based on the above criterion, the following derivatives were selected: futures contracts on WIG20 (index futures), Telekomunikacja Polska S.A. (equity futures contract), US dollar/Polish Zloty (currency futures), and index participation units on Warsaw Stock Exchange WIG20 Index.

Tables 7.2 and 7.3 present the results of all the tests on the daily and weekly rates of return on futures contracts on WIG20

No	Derivative	Basis date of data	No. of daily data	Quotation unit	Multiplier used to determine contract value	Minimum steps of quotation	Value of minimum step of quotation	Commission on the quotation units (%)
Index futures contracts								
1	FW20	6.3.1998	1337	index point	10	1 index point	10 PLN	2
2	FMID	18.2.2002	349	index point	10	1 index point	10 PLN	2
3	FTEC	1.8.2000	731	index point	10	1 index point	10 PLN	2
Equity futures contracts								
4	FAGO	23.10.2001	395	PLN	200	0.05 PLN	10 PLN	0.1
5	FBPH	19.3.2002	265	PLN	50	0.05 PLN	2.5 PLN	0.4
6	FBRE	22.10.2001	392	PLN	100	0.05 PLN	5 PLN	0.2
7	FELE	22.1.2001	483	PLN	3000	0.05 PLN	15 PLN	0.067
8	FKGH	22.10.2001	428	PLN	500	0.05 PLN	25 PLN	0.04
9	FPEO	22.10.2001	426	PLN	100	0.05 PLN	5 PLN	0.2
10	FPKN	22.1.2001	616	PLN	500	0.05 PLN	25 PLN	0.04
11	FPKM	22.1.2001	390	PLN	100	0.05 PLN	5 PLN	0.2
12	FTPS	22.1.2001	618	PLN	500	0.05 PLN	25 PLN	0.04
Currency future contracts								
13	FEUR	31.5.1999	1001	PLN/100 EUR	10000	0.01/100 EUR	1 PLN	0.2
14	FUSD	29.9.1998	1147	PLN/100 USD	100000	0.01/100 USD	1 PLN	0.2
Index participation units on WIG20								
15	MW20	26.11.2001	398	PLN	0.1	0.01 PLN	0.01 PLN	0.5

Source: Individual work based on the trading rules for index and equity futures contracts on the Warsaw Stock Exchange

Table 7.2 FW20 results, percentage daily rate of return

			Buy and hold strategy	Tested investment strategies								
				I	II	III	IV	V	VI	VII	VIII	IX
Volume and type of optimum strategy parameters		Type	–	E	VAR	–	W	–	S	E	–	–
		Opt1	–	2	9	49	22	22	13	39	7	50
		Opt2	–	13	6	100	–	–	17	–	50	16
		Opt3	–	–	–	–	–	–	15	–	–	3
Total profit of strategy*			−447	3403	3580	1653	3142	2502	3363	2002	2671	2978
Number of transactions			1	211	5	39	271	269	241	167	355	153
I_0 = value of the contract	Strategy	$\overline{R}$	−0.0012	0.1539	0.1679	0.0836	0.1511	0.1087	0.1485	0.1068	0.1244	0.1390
		S	1.981	1.9466	1.7228	1.913	1.9477	1.9494	1.9146	1.9275	1.9594	1.9204
Rate of return improvement %			–	–	–	–	–	–	–	–	–	–
Risk reduction %			–	−1.74	−13.03	−3.43	−1.68	−1.60	−3.35	−2.70	−1.09	−3.06
I_0** = Deposit	Strategy	$\overline{R}$	−0.0279	1.1979	1.4809	0.6319	1.1758	0.7989	0.9555	0.9948	0.9371	1.0076
		S	18.5092	17.575	16.337	17.236	17.607	17.572	17.260	17.326	17.723	17.320
Rate of return improvement %			–	–	–	–	–	–	–	–	–	–
Risk reduction %			–	−5.05	−11.73	−6.88	−4.88	−5.06	−6.75	−6.39	−4.25	−6.43

Notes: * in the quotation units; ** initial investment.

Source: Individual survey on the basis of the optimization tests in the MetaStock 8.0

Table 7.3 FW20 results, percentage weekly rate of return

		Buy and hold strategy	Tested investment systems								
			I	II	III	IV	V	VI	VII	VIII	IX
Volume and type of	Type	–	E	VAR	–	W	–	S	E	–	–
optimum strategy	Opt1	–	2	9	49	22	22	13	39	7	50
parameters	Opt2	–	13	6	100	–	–	17	–	50	16
	Opt3	–	–	–	–	–	–	15	–	–	3
Total profit of strategy*		−447	3403	3580	1653	3142	2502	3363	2002	2671	2978
Number of transactions		1	211	5	39	271	269	241	167	355	153
I_0 = value of the contract Strategy	$\overline{R}$	−0.0127	0.7732	0.8393	0.4164	0.7594	0.5456	0.7250	0.5402	0.6261	0.6785
	S	4.8453	3.8176	3.9293	4.2627	3.9031	3.9091	4.1644	4.0818	4.0228	3.7781
Rate of return improvement %		–	–	–	–	–	–	–	–	–	–
Risk reduction %		–	−21.2	−18.9	−12.0	−19.4	−19.3	−14.1	−15.8	−17.0	−22.0
I_0** = Deposit Strategy	$\overline{R}$	−0.4524	6.0201	7.3331	3.1747	5.8864	4.0095	4.7660	5.0757	4.5679	4.9587
			2		1	4	5	3	6	4	6
	S	43.3433	34.682	36.250	38.022	34.436	35.786	38.238	36.034	35.829	34.711
			4	3	2	4	8	7	1	6	3
Rate of return improvement %		–	–	–	–	–	–	–	–	–	–
Risk reduction %		–	−20.0	−16.4	−12.3	−20.5	−17.4	−11.8	−16.9	−17.3	−19.9

Notes: * in the quotation units; ** initial investment.
Sources: Individual survey on the basis of the optimization tests in the MetaStock 8.0

respectively. The tables also provide information on the value and type of optimal parameters for tested strategies that were considered in the test, and the total profit and number of concluded transactions for tested strategies. The results for the remaining contracts are not presented here owing to the limited scope of this chapter.

The results show that the majority of technical analysis strategies generate significantly higher profit (total profit, in the course of simulation) than the control strategy (buy and hold strategy). Even more important is the fact that the average rate of return of the strategies is higher than the rate of return of control strategy in almost all cases. The only exception to this is the daily and weekly rate of return for FUSD (future contract on US dollar) in the case of the fifth strategy. The scope for improvement of the average rate of return for all tested strategies in comparison to the control strategy is from −96 per cent (two cases with a negative value) to 650 per cent. (The above calculations were not carried out for FW20 (future contract on WIG20 index) and FTPS (future contract on TPS) as the average rates of return in the case of control strategy were below zero, whereas for tested strategies they were above zero.)

Moreover, for the vast majority of tested strategies, it was found that their risks measured by their standard deviation were approximately equal to or lower than the risk of the control strategy. The extent by which risks have been reduced was between −24 per cent to +3 per cent. Out of the 64 cases that were considered, only 7 cases showed an increase in standard deviation in comparison with the control strategy. It was also noticed that the extent by which the standard deviation of weekly rates of return declined was considerably higher than in the standard deviation of daily rates of return. Based on the above observation, it is not possible to conclude that the increase in rates of return was related to the increase in risks of the strategies.

The next observation was related to differences in the average rates of return and risks of two different types of initial investment. It was noted that in strategies where deposit was the initial source of investment, there was a much higher rate of return, and a proportionally higher standard deviation. That was related to the effect of financial leverage effect.

Differences between optimized parameters

Analysis of the results presented in Tables 7.2 and 7.3 provides more information about the volume and type of optimized parameters. In each strategy, the optimized parameters were considerably different from the initial values of the instruments that were earlier set by the issuer. This result shows that despite the fact that, initially, there might have been significant differences in characters and variability of security prices, the comprehensive optimization of a wide range of instruments can reveal the individual, character of price changes.

This observation is crucial in modelling investment strategies on the basis of past data. The data optimization results of this study point out that the most profitable investment strategies are those that are based on different theoretical assumptions. Moreover, even parameters that were optimized in accordance with the same strategy generated a totally different outcome. To summarize, we can say that differences in the sets of optimized parameters described, indicate the necessity for continuous improvement of techniques defined initially by TA pioneers corresponding to ongoing changes in the market situation.

It is worth mentioning some of the reasons for the minimal acknowledgement of technical analysis in the academic world. Criticism of technical analysis emerges, mostly, because theorists treat technical analysis as methods of reading charts of prices in order to make buy/sell decisions. The method used in this study, by focusing on visual analysis of prices and charts, ignores mathematical methods that interpret the buy/sell signals and makes decisions accordingly, without any subjective evaluation of situation. The presented study, however, has shown how some of the tools of technical analysis can be used in designing investment strategies.

Results of the study on market efficiency

In order to formulate the results of this study, it is first useful to outline the four main features of an efficient market.[16] These are:

1 Prices of securities respond immediately to new information and according to the specific features of the security;
2 Changes in security prices are random;
3 Simulation tests that are based on defined transaction formulas should not have abnormal rates of return;
4 Qualified investors, who trade in groups or individually, are not able to gain higher rates of return than the average ones.

There is no reason to reject the weak-form of EMH, as long as the market fulfils the first and third conditions. The results of this study shake the foundations of the third condition and tend to dispute the validity of the first. If prices react immediately to new information, then the given information should be included in the price level at once. Thus, it makes it impossible to model investment strategies that are based on historical data and yet generate abnormal rates of return. Therefore, the first condition can only be fulfilled if the third condition holds, but the problem is that the validity of the third condition itself is under the question.

On the basis of the results of this study, it is possible to draw a few general conclusions about weak-form market efficiency, and possibly design a 'beat the market' investment strategy. The conclusions are:

- The tests conducted on listed futures contracts on the WSE weaken the validity of weak-form EMH.
- Efficiency tests showed that it is possible to use past prices and methods used in technical analysis to design an investment strategy that can generate abnormal profits compared with what can be achieved under the control strategies.
- Expanding the market environment by adding new institutions and individuals to the market, and changing the proportions of participants in the structure of the market, is a factor that can influence the process and shape of continuous change in prices. An example of this has been presented here, where the best strategy was identified through progressive change of the optimized parameters.
- High level of diversification of the optimized parameters (i.e. different best combination of parameters of given investment strategy for different future contracts) revealed a variety of prices and characters of particular futures contracts. This may be the reason why 'negative' results were obtained in some of the tests of market efficiency, where all instruments quoted on the market were considered as a whole, and parameters of particular methods were calculated as an average of the whole market.
- The investment strategies do not generate similar results in every market. In other words, it is not possible to apply them to different types of markets (in terms of geographical locations, level of development and type of basic instruments traded in the market).

Inevitably there would be a need for modification and adjustment of signals and their parameters to the different market environments.

While examining the validity of weak-form EMH, it is worth recalling that if the set of information that determines the semi-strong form of EMH is contained in the set of information that determines strong-form EMH, then any conclusion that shakes the foundation of weak-form efficiency, also strongly calls to question the validity of the other forms of EMH.

Reasons for deviation from EMH

At this stage it is worth mentioning some of the factors that can cause deviation from the EMH:

- Developments within the capital markets in terms of changes in the structure and features of institutions and instruments. These developments can automatically have important implications for efficiency and their impacts have not yet fully examined.
- The character of market trend in the course of testing is very important, as it can significantly influence the results of any technical analysis, in particular in the case of strong price trends.
- The majority of studies on market efficiency tend to use a control strategy, the results of which constitute the base of comparison of other tested strategies. In studies that examine weak-form efficiency, it is usually the buy and hold strategy that is sensitive to the beginning and ending moment of the tests. Any change in these can alter the results.

Conclusion

The results of this study showed that it is possible to create investment strategies with abnormal gains on the basis of a historical set of information. Though this study may not be sufficient to conclusively reject weak-form EMH, it can still shake the foundations of the hypothesis.

It is true to say that the existence or absence of weak-form efficiency can have important implications for the other forms of efficiency. It would have been very interesting if one could have conclusively rejected weak-form EMH, as it would have undoubtedly had important implications for the other two hypotheses. The last issue is related to the volatile character of market prices, which makes it necessary to optimize individual parameters of particular instruments in any investment strategy in order to create a highly profitable strategy of 'beat the market'.

Notes

1. William F. Sharpe (1995) *Investments* (London: Prentice Hall).
2. H. Roberts (1959) 'Statistical versus Clinical Prediction of the Stock Market', Unpublished manuscript (Chicago: University of Chicago, CRSP).
3. E.F. Fama (1970) 'Efficient Capital Markets: A Review of Theory and Empirical Work', *Journal of Finance*, 25, 383–417.
4. *New Palgrave Dictionary of Money and Finance* (1992) (London: Macmillan).
5. That kind of survey verified the situation, in which the specified month in the year, week in the month, day in the week or hour in the day generated an abnormal rate of return.
6. Brzeszczyński Janusz and Robert Kelm (2002) *Ekonometryczne modele rynków finansowych* (Warsaw: WIG-Press), 40–1.
7. Long position means the purchase of futures contracts (see Hull, 1998).
8. Short position means the sale of futures contracts (see Hull, 1998).
9. http://www.paritech.com/education/technical/indicators/trend/movavg-3.asp
10. http://www.paritech.com/education/technical/indicators/trend/movavg-6.asp
11. In the text, we used the following abbreviations for the different types of average: E – exponential moving average, S – simple moving average, T – time series moving average, TRI – triangular moving average, VAR – variable moving average, VOL – volume adjusted moving average, W-weighted moving average.
12. J.J. Murphy (1999) *Analiza techniczna rynków finansowych* (Warsaw: WIG-Press), 183–6.
13. Under market categories impetus can be defined as the change of the price of a given instrument in the specified time (see Etzkorn, 1999).
14. Etzkorn M. (1999) *Osciylatory* (Warsaw: WIG-Press), 106–7.
15. Etzkorn M. (1999) *Oscylatory* (Warsaw: WIG-Press), 27–9.
16. Robert A. Haugen (1996) 'The January Effect: Still there after all these years', *Financial Analyst Journal*, 52, 27–31.

References

Appel, G. (1985) '*The Moving Average Convergence/Divergence Trading Method*, Advanced Version, Scientific Investment System (Ontario: Traders Press, June 1985).

Ariel, R.A. (1987) 'A Monthly Effect in Stock Returns', *Journal of Financial Economics*, 18, 161–74.
Basu, S. (1977) 'Investments Performance of Common Stock in Relation to Their Price-Earnings Ratio: A Test of the EMH', *Journal of Finance*, 32, 663–82.
Banz, R. (1981) 'The Relationship between Return and Market Value of Common Stocks', *Journal of Financial Economics*, 9(1), 3–18.
Black, F. and Scholes, M. (1972) 'The Valuation of Options Contracts and a Test of Market Efficiency', *Journal of Finance*, 27, 399–417.
Brzeszczyński, Janusz and Kelm, Robert (2002) *Ekonometryczne modele rynków finansowych* (Warsaw: WIG-Press).
Campbell, J.Y., Lo, A.W. and MacKinlay, A.C. (1997) *The Econometrics of Financial Markets* (Princeton: Princeton University Press).
Cootner, P. (1964) *The Random Character of Stock Market Prices* (Cambridge, MA: MIT).
Cornell, B. and Roll, R. (1981) 'Strategies for Pair-Wise Competitions in Market and Organizations', *Bell Journal of Economics*, 12(1), 201–13.
Czekaj, J., Woś, M. and Żarnowski, J. (2001) *Efektywność giełdowego rynku akcji w Polsce*, Wydawnictwo Naukowe PWN, Warszawa.
Etzkorn, M. (1999) *Oscylatory* (Warsaw: WIG-Press), 27–9.
Fama, E.F. (1998) 'Market Efficiency, Long-Term Returns and Behavioural Finance', *Journal of Financial Economics*, 49, 283–306.
Fama, E.F. (1991) 'Efficient Capital Markets II', *Journal of Finance*, 46, 1575–617.
Fama, E.F. (1970) 'Efficient Capital Markets: A Review of Theory and Empirical Work', *Journal of Finance*, 25, 383–417.
Fama, E., French, K., Jensen, M. and Roll, R. (1969) 'The Adjustment of Stock Prices to New Information', *International Economic Review*, 10, 1–21.
French, K.R. (1980) 'Stock Returns and the Weekend Effect', *Journal of Financial Economics*, 8, 55–69.
Friend, I., Brown, F., Herman, E. and Vickers, D. (1962) *A Study of Mutual Funds* (Washington, DC: US Government Printing Office).
Harris, L. (1986) 'A Transaction Data Study of Weekly and Intradaily Patterns in Stock Returns', *Journal of Financial Economics*, 16, 99–117.
Haugen, Robert A. (1999) *Nowa nauka o finansach: Przeciw efektywności rynku* (Warsaw: WIG-Press).
Haugen, Robert A. (1996) 'The January Effect: Still There after All These Years', *Financial Analysts Journal*, 52, 27–31.
Hull, J. (1998) *Kontrakty terminowe i opcje. Wprowadzenie* (Warsaw: WIG-Press).
Jajuga, K. (2000) *Metody ekonometryczne i statystyczne w analizie rynku kapitałowego*, (Wrocław: Wydawnictwo Akademii Ekonomicznej we Wrocławiu).
Jaffe, J. (1974) 'Special Information and Insider Trading', *Journal of Business*, 47, 410–28.
Jensen, M. (1969) 'Risk, the Pricing of Capital Assets, and the Evaluation of Investment Portfolios', *Journal of Business*, 42(2), 167–247.
Keim, D.B. (1983) 'Size-related Anomalies and Stock Return Seasonality: Further Empirical Evidence', *Journal of Financial Economics*, 12, 13–32.

Kraus, A. and Stoll, H. (1972) 'Price Impacts of Block Trading on the NYSE', *Journal of Finance*, 27(3), 569–88.
Lane, G. and George, C. (1986) *Lane's Stochastics, Technical Analysis of Stock and Commodities, Investment Techniques*, vol. 2 (Jack K. Huston, ed.), 87–90.
Le Beau, C. and Lucas, D.W. (1998) *Komputerowa analiza rynków terminowych* (Warsaw: WIG-Press).
Malkiel, B.G. (2003) *Błądząc po Wall Street, 2003, Dlaczego nie można wygrać z rynkiem* (Warsaw: WIG-Press).
Murphy, J.J. (1999) *Analiza techniczna rynków finansowych* (Warsaw: WIG-Press).
Pring, M.J. (1998) *Podstawy analizy technicznej* (Warsaw: WIG-Press).
Roberts, H. (1959) 'Statistical versus Clinical Prediction of the Stock Market', Unpublished manuscript, CRSP (Chicago: University of Chicago).
Rozeff, M.S. and Kinney, W.R. (1976) 'Capital Market Seasonality: The Case of Stock Returns', *Journal of Financial Economics*, 3, 379–402.
Sharpe, W.F. (1995) *Investments* (London: Prentice Hall).
Szyszka, A. (2003) *Efektywność giełdy papierów wartościowych w Warszawie na tle rynków dojrzałych* (Poznań: Wydawnictwo Akademii Ekonomicznej).
Szyszka, A. (2000) 'Skuteczność reguły filtrów na polskim rynku kapitałowym', *Nasz Rynek Kapitałowy*, 6, 51–4.
Wilder, J.W. (1978) *New Concepts in Technical Trading Systems* (Greensboro: Trend Research).

Index